MOUNTAIN WALKS
YR WYDDFA
SNOWDON

MOUNTAIN WALKS
YR WYDDFA SNOWDON

15 ROUTES TO ENJOY ON AND AROUND SNOWDON

First published in 2024 by Vertebrate Publishing.

 Vertebrate Publishing
Omega Court, 352 Cemetery Road, Sheffield S11 8FT, United Kingdom.
www.adventurebooks.com

A CIP catalogue record for this book is available from the British Library.

ISBN 978-1-83981-202-6 (Paperback)
ISBN 978-1-83981-203-3 (Ebook)

Front cover: View to Yr Wyddfa from Llyn Llydaw. © John Coefield.
Back cover: Descending past Castell y Gwynt with Yr Wyddfa in the distance.
Photography by Kate Worthington unless otherwise credited.

 All maps reproduced by permission of Ordnance Survey on behalf of The Controller of His Majesty's Stationery Office. © Crown Copyright. AC0000809882

Design and production by Jane Beagley
www.adventurebooks.com

Printed and bound in Europe by Latitude Press.

Vertebrate Publishing is committed to printing on paper from sustainable sources.

MOUNTAIN WALKS
YR WYDDFA
SNOWDON

15 ROUTES TO ENJOY ON AND AROUND SNOWDON

KATE WORTHINGTON

Vertebrate Publishing, Sheffield
www.adventurebooks.com

/ CONTENTS

Download the
Mountain Walks Yr Wyddfa/Snowdon
GPX files from
www.adventurebooks.com/MWYW-GPX

ROUTE GRADES
Easy ●○○○
Medium ●●○○
Hard ●●●○
Full-on ●●●●

/ INTRODUCTION

This collection of walks celebrates the grandeur and contrasting character of Yr Wyddfa and its surrounding landscapes. Set within Eryri National Park, the Yr Wyddfa massif and its many valley communities, delicate habitats and wildlife, people and history offers the opportunity to explore, enjoy and connect with a very special place. Designated a National Nature Reserve, the rugged mountain shapes of Yr Wyddfa and the neighbouring summits were born from intense geological forces acting on the Earth's tectonic plates over 625 million years ago. Fast-forward to 2.6 million years ago and glacial activity had started to carve out the landforms we see today – high mountain cwms and glacial llyns, narrow ridges and steep, scree-covered slopes. The environs of Yr Wyddfa have provided natural resources and shelter for humans since the end of the last ice age about 12,000 years ago.

The routes described offer a wide variety of ways to enjoy Yr Wyddfa's landscapes, catering for long mountain days as well as shorter walks suitable for families or unsettled weather conditions. Perhaps you'll feel inspired to learn more about a particular village or valley, Welsh summit name, historical or natural feature. There are some classic routes here, as well as some alternative ideas to freshen up your planning. Many visitors to Eryri already 'know' and appreciate the special qualities of Yr Wyddfa, but this book offers additional discoveries and insights into this much-loved mountain massif.

Mwynhewch eich cerdded ar Yr Wyddfa.

Kate Worthington

Y Lliwedd and Yr Wyddfa from Llyn Llydaw. © *John Coefield*

ACKNOWLEDGEMENTS

Diolch yn fawr iawn/Thank you very much to Vertebrate Publishing for brilliant advice and support. I am always thankful to my husband, Ross, and daughter, Libby, for accompanying (and accommodating) my mountain escapes and quiet writing times. And always to Nonny-dog, a wonderful companion in the Eryri hills.

ABOUT THE WALKS

Most of the upland terrain on Yr Wyddfa and its surrounding summits is owned and managed by various estates, farms and organisations, including the National Trust and Eryri National Park. The Countryside and Rights of Way Act of 2000 (CRoW Act, sometimes referred to as the 'right to roam') came into effect in Wales in May 2005, and this granted legal access for those on foot to enjoy exploring 'access land'. Given that there are also a huge number of historical public rights of way (public footpaths or public bridleways) within and outside the 'access land', there is a wealth of terrain to enjoy and explore in this area.

For clarity, ease of use and planning, the walks described in this guidebook usually follow established public rights of way, where you have the legal right to 'pass and repass along the way'. Some of the routes use permissive paths, where a landowner has granted access for users, but this is not defined by law and walkers must adhere to waymarkers or signs placed by the landowner (for example, the National Trust). Sections of walks in upland terrain follow established paths over CRoW access land and some of these routes are clearer than others on the ground, depending on the popularity of the area. Some routes over access land are mapped and some are not; this may also depend on what type of mapping you're using.

The timings quoted for each walk are quite generous, assuming an average walking pace of 3–4km/h (2–3mph), which also factors in time for breaks, photos and the effort of ascent/terrain as applicable. The 'running' times quoted reflect the fact that a runner may move more efficiently over most terrain, but will still walk many of the ascents, moving at an average speed of 5–8km/h (3–5mph).

NAVIGATION

The mapping and descriptions in this guidebook are intended for planning and information; you will need to use additional mapping and navigation methods while walking, either a hard-copy map and compass, or a good quality online mapping app (such as OS Maps, Gaia GPS, OutdoorActive, or Topo GPS, as well as OS Locate) on a mobile phone or GPS unit. Both require practice; understanding maps and symbols and orienting yourself from them is a useful skill to learn; there are many tutorial videos online that can help with this.

While many mountain users access route and mapping information on mobile devices or GPS units, be aware that digital mapping sources can drain your mobile phone/GPS unit's battery; ensure that you carry a hard-copy map which does not rely on having mobile phone signal and will increase your ability to see the bigger picture. Pack a portable power bank to recharge your device on the hill, especially if you also want to use your phone to make calls or take photos.

Using a map and compass will increase your accuracy and confidence when navigating in poor visibility, especially when departing from summits. Many walkers have descended Yr Wyddfa in completely the wrong direction due to not checking their location and direction of travel before setting off.

The walks all appear on the following maps:

- **Ordnance Survey Explorer OL17 Snowdon/Yr Wyddfa (Conwy Valley/Dyffryn Conwy) – 1:25,000**

  A large-scale map with lots of detail suitable for walking. Four centimetres on the map represent one kilometre in real life. These maps come in a paper or weatherproof laminated format and come with a link to a digital version to use in the OS Maps app.

- **Harvey Maps/BMC British Mountain Map – Snowdonia North/Gogledd Eryri – 1:40,000**

  This map is slightly smaller scale, but is excellent for walking and planning routes, due to the visual use of colours to denote mountain heights/terrain. Two and a half centimetres on the map represent one kilometre in real life. These maps are printed on waterproof paper and are very light to carry.

| SAFETY & WELL-BEING

Keeping safe and well in upland terrain starts with an appropriate plan that suits both you and your group and the forecast weather and mountain conditions, and allows for enjoyment and adventure along the way. Bear in mind that a robust plan will allow for changes; you shouldn't be locked into a single objective, as outside factors may influence your day. These factors might include changeable weather and how it affects you on the hill, how you/the group are feeling given the terrain or effort, your estimated/actual speed of travel, the length of daylight hours, parking and access/public transport times, what clothing you're wearing/carrying and even how much food/drink you have with you. Let someone outside your group know where you're going and what time you're expecting to be back down (and let them know when you're off the hill to prevent them from worrying). When planning your day, check out *www.adventuresmart.uk/wales* for helpful tips and reminders of what factors to consider. #BeAdventureSmart

If you're unsure about aspects of your planned route, do some research online to find out more or ask for advice in local accommodation or shops to fill your knowledge gaps. Ensure that you have enough protective clothing and equipment for the forecasted weather and get an updated forecast appropriate for your planned route. The Met Office provides mountain summit (Yr Wyddfa/Snowdon, or Glyder Fawr, for example) and mountain area-specific (Eryri/Snowdonia) forecasts which provide data for the summit height, which will usually be very different to valley level weather, since the air is colder the higher you ascend. It's no good looking at a weather forecast for Llanberis if you're walking to the summit of Yr Wyddfa as they are two very different forecasts.

Don't underestimate how much food and drink you might need for longer/ higher outings, especially when walking with children. Plan to snack/drink every 30 to 40 minutes to keep energy levels high and avoid tired limbs or slowing down. The walking times in this guidebook include some time to stop to eat or drink, but always keep an eye on your walking pace and how this compares to your plans. Are the weather conditions or terrain affecting your speed? Do you still have time to complete your planned objective or should you shorten your route or turn back earlier than planned? Never be afraid to check on your group, check your map, check your watch and change plans if necessary, especially if you can see or feel bad weather arriving quicker than forecasted.

KIT & COMFORT

When choosing clothes and kit for mountain walks, think about the principles of comfort and protection. Avoid cotton clothing, as these lose their insulating properties when damp with sweat or wet with rain. Comfortable, synthetic walking trousers or leggings are a good option, as is a synthetic top or base layer over which a warm layer can be added. Don't forget to protect your arms, head and neck in very sunny weather.

Take a rucksack containing an extra warm layer (or two if it's very cold), a pair of warm gloves and a hat, a zippable, waterproof jacket with a large hood, and waterproof trousers that you can pull over your walking trousers/leggings. Layering several thinner layers is more flexible than wearing a very thick ski jacket or similar.

Your rucksack should also contain food, drink, a map, a phone charger and power bank, and a waterproof bag to keep everything in. You might also wish to include a head torch (and spare batteries), depending on the time of year/time of day that you're planning to walk, a small first aid kit, and an emergency group shelter that you can sit on or in for lunch breaks or use for emergency shelter in the event of an unforeseen situation or injury. When packing your kit, ask yourself

'Can I keep myself comfortable, warm and dry even if I'm walking much more slowly than planned or if I've stopped completely, in a variety of weather and mountain conditions?'

For some of the routes, a pair of trail/off-road trainers with an aggressive sole may be sufficient; it is best to avoid flat-soled trainers as these don't provide enough grip on rock or in wet conditions. Walking boots offer good ankle support and excellent grip, but make sure you get used to wearing them before a long day out.

Ticks can carry Lyme disease; they lurk in the bracken and long vegetation in summer so walking trousers are advised during this season. Walk in the middle of paths and avoid unnecessarily walking through bushy vegetation or long grass. Advice for preventing tick bites and tick removal is available here: *www.lymediseaseaction.org.uk*

Check a mountain weather forecast to ensure that you pack the kit you need (including precautionary extras) and make sure you wear a watch so you can keep track of time. Always 'Stop and Be Bothered' to change/add a layer rather than ignoring what your body or the weather are telling you.

| MOUNTAIN RESCUE

Mountain Rescue England and Wales is a charity that relies on volunteer time, donations and fundraising to operate. The walks covered in this guidebook are located in Northern Eryri, which is covered by the Llanberis Mountain Rescue Team and Ogwen Valley Mountain Rescue Team. Visit *www.mountain.rescue.org.uk* for more information.

Many mountain rescue calls are made when people find themselves in exposed conditions in poor weather or darkness, lost or overcome by fatigue or cold/wet/hot weather. Making appropriate plans and amending them if needed, as well as eating adequate food and taking enough kit, clothing and mapping will help to safeguard against things unravelling during the day.

That said, mountain rescue teams advise that you should always call if you need assistance. They can sometimes provide advice over the telephone to help you take the best action on the hill for you and your group.

What To Do in an Emergency

If you or someone else is in need of emergency assistance in the mountains, dial **999** (or **112**) and ask for **POLICE** and then **MOUNTAIN RESCUE**. This relies on you having mobile phone signal and a charged phone buttery, and being able to give the relevant details over the phone when asked (location, name/s and details of people affected, what has happened and your contact details). You may be

On Glyder Fach, with Yr Wyddfa in the distance. © *John Coefield*

asked to stay in position or in signal range so the mountain rescue team can call you back. Keep yourself and others warm and insulated from the ground and the weather. Put on layers, eat something for energy and sit out of the wind on a bag or clothing.

Emergency Rescue By SMS Text

In the UK you can contact the emergency services by SMS text. While this service is primarily intended for those with hearing or speech difficulties, it can be useful if you have low battery or intermittent signal. You need to register your phone beforehand by texting **'register'** to **999** and then following the instructions in the reply. ***www.emergencysms.net***

| BEHAVIOUR & RESPECTING THE ENVIRONMENT

Due to the popularity of Yr Wyddfa and its surrounding areas, it is imperative that you take the time to plan visits to maximise enjoyment and safety, and avoid having a negative impact on the natural environment and local communities. During busy holiday times, it is usually inconsiderate parking, inappropriate behaviour in public spaces (shouting, loud music, taking illegal drugs) and discarded food remains/litter that create the highest impact, as well as dogs causing worry or injury to local livestock. These problems can all be ameliorated by modifying your behaviour and attitudes in the light of the surrounding communities and landscape. For further information, see ***www.naturalresources.wales/days-out/the-countryside-codes***

A summary of the Countryside Code in Wales is below:

Respect everyone
- be considerate to those living in, working in and enjoying the countryside
- leave gates and property as you find them
- do not block access to gateways or driveways when parking
- be nice, say hello, share the space
- follow local signs and keep to marked paths unless wider access is available

Protect the environment
- take your litter home – leave no trace of your visit (including fruit peel)
- do not light fires and only have BBQs where signs say you can
- always keep your dogs under control and in sight
- dog poo – bag it and bin it in any public waste bin or take it home
- care for nature – do not cause damage or disturbance (do not move stones, damage ruins or plants and trees, or disturb wildlife)

Enjoy the outdoors
- check your route (make sure you have the relevant maps) and local conditions
- plan your adventure – know what to expect and what you can do
- enjoy your visit, have fun, make a memory

Know the signs and symbols of the countryside
- Public Footpath, Public Bridleway
- Restricted Byway, Byway Open to All Traffic, Permissive Path
- Open Access Land, End of Open Access Land

WALKING WITH YOUR DOG

Shared adventures with our canine companions can be wonderful. However, given the delicate balance between outdoor recreation and farming on and around Yr Wyddfa, it's essential to know how to look after our dogs, both for their health and safety and for the well-being of other people and animals around us, including grazing livestock and local wildlife.

Legally on a Public Right of Way an owner does not have to keep a dog on a lead, as long as the dog remains under 'close control'. However, the advice from Eryri National Park is to keep dogs on a short lead. On Open Access Land, there is a legal requirement to keep dogs on a short lead between 1 March and 31 July to safeguard breeding ground nesting birds and livestock, and owners must always be in control of their dog. Farmers have the legal right to destroy any dog that is causing worry or harm to livestock.

Dog poo needs to be bagged up and disposed of in an appropriate bin as it can contain bacteria and parasites which are a health risk to grazing animals, people and dogs.

Be wary of how your dog will behave around livestock. Keep your distance from cows and horses where possible, especially if the animals have their young with them. If animals closely follow or chase you, let go of your dog's lead and focus on your own safety.

/ HOW TO USE THIS BOOK

Use this book for inspiration, to improve your knowledge, find out local information and as part of your planning process. The maps in this book are the same as the Ordnance Survey Explorer OL17 map described on page ix, but you should always take a separate map out with you in case you need to refer to the wider area around the walk. The text descriptions allow you to work your way through the route visually with a map before you set out, as well as providing a reference when you're walking. Familiarise yourself with the symbols used on the map and consider possible escape routes in case you need to retrace your steps or lose height to escape poor weather.

The descriptions of the walks in the Mountain Walks series as …

Easy	●○○○
Medium	●●○○
Hard	●●●○
Full-on	●●●●

… do not just relate to the distance of the route. The gradings have been reached by considering a mixture of distance, ascent profile, type of terrain and technicality, and how easy the route might be to navigate in poor weather.

Follow the advice above about choosing equipment, using mountain-specific weather forecasts and how to look after yourself and your party to maximise your enjoyment and safety. Additional information can be found via the websites listed, which offer further opportunities to increase your knowledge and confidence in planning and enjoying walks in the mountainous terrain on and around Yr Wyddfa.

Map Key

| **S** | **2** | ↗ | 52 |
| Route starting point | Route marker | Direction arrow | Additional grid line numbers to aid navigation |

| WELSH LANGUAGE & PLACE NAMES

This book refers to Eryri National Park rather than Snowdonia, and Yr Wyddfa in preference to Snowdon. This reflects a decisive move by Eryri National Park to celebrate the integration of these historic Welsh names into general discussion and communication. The mapping of the area also uses the Welsh language and Welsh place names, providing a contextual introduction to the language of Wales.

aber – estuary, confluence
afon – river
allt – wood, slope
bach/fach – small
blaen – head of a valley
brith – coarse, speckled
bryn – hill
bwlch – pass or gap
cae – field
caer/gaer – fort, fortified camp
capel – chapel
carn/garn – cairn or pile of stones
carreg/garreg – stone
castell – castle
cefn – ridge
coch/goch – red
coed – wood
craig/graig – crag
cwm – valley
dwr – water
dyffryn – valley
eglwys – church
ffordd – road
ffynnon – well or spring
glan/lan – bank or shore
glyn – deep valley
gwaun/waun – moorland or meadow
gwern – place where alders grow, swamp
hen – old
isaf – lower/lowest

llan – church, sacred enclosure
llwyn – bush or grove
llyn – lake
maen – stone
maes – field
mawr/fawr – big
mochyn (pl. *moch*) – pig
moel/foel – bare hill
mynydd – mountain
nant – stream
ogof – cave
pant – hollow
pen – top or end
pentre – village
plas – hall, mansion
pont/bont – bridge
porth – harbour
pwll – pool
rhiw – slope
rhos – moorland
rhyd – ford
saeth (pl. *saethau*) – arrow
tan/dan – below
tref/dref – homestead or town
twll – hole
ty – house
uchaf – upper
y, yr – the
ynys – island

4.5km / 2.8 miles

01 / CHWAREL DINORWIG

A dramatic introductory walk to Dinorwig quarries. Though short in distance, it packs in glorious mountain views, intrigue and a lovingly curated gnome garden … surprise!

/ ESSENTIAL INFO

GRADE ●○○○○
DISTANCE **4.5KM/2.8 MILES**
ASCENT **230M**
TIME **1.5 HRS (WALKER)/45 MINS (RUNNER)**
START/FINISH **NATIONAL SLATE MUSEUM PAY & DISPLAY CAR PARK**
START GRID REF **SH 585 604**
START GPS **53.1218, -4.1153**
OS MAP **OL17 SNOWDON/YR WYDDFA (1:25,000)**

/ OVERVIEW

Chwarel Dinorwig (Dinorwig Quarry) is part of a new UNESCO World Heritage Site in north-west Wales, celebrating the industrial slate landscape of the area. This slate story plays out on the impressive slopes that rise above the villages of Llanberis, Nant Peris and Deiniolen. These areas were operational from the late 1700s right up until 1969; cavernous pits were excavated, quarried and then abandoned, linked by high galleries and train systems on steep inclines. This walk offers a short adventure into this industrial world, where the haunting remains of quarry machinery and buildings will inspire the imagination of walkers of all ages. Once through the quarry areas, look out for the impressive local gnomes, and the delightful native oak woodland of Coed Dinorwig.

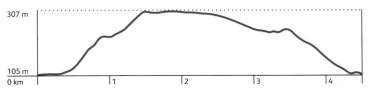

View to Yr Wyddfa from Chwarel Dinorwig. © Evan Davies

Mountain goats in Chwarel Dinorwig. © Evan Davies

/ DIRECTIONS

S Exit the National Slate Museum car park via the road leading back to Llanberis and follow this for a few hundred metres until you reach a mini-roundabout, near the entrance to Electric Mountain, the slightly unimaginable hydroelectric power station inside the mountain above Llanberis run by First Hydro Company (FHC). FHC also owns much of the quarry land surrounding this route. As you approach the roundabout, **look left** for a small opening in a slate wall, and a stepped path leading up and away from the road. This is a steep start, following a stepped path on a wooded slope initially, then using a narrow, walled, zigzag path to ascend a huge pile of slate waste! Breathe a sigh of relief as the path flattens out at the site of an old metal bridge, where you can see an old drum wheel at the top of an incline on your left. Ascend for another 150m on a twisty path through trees to a path junction with old buildings on your right.

2 Take the path on your **right** that stays level, passing through the remains of the old barracks. After this, the route **turns left** and ascends again, using an old tram incline to access the highest point of this walk, at 300m. From the incline, view the expanse of Chwarel Dinorwig above, as well as some of the modern infrastructure of the FHC power station below. At the top of the incline, exit through a metal swing gate into a large, flat area, home to the large 'Mill No. 3,' a slate splitting mill. **Turn left** from the metal gate and walk to the end of the viewing platform. Retrace your steps towards the old slate mill, then **turn left** and follow a wide, slate track for 600m before exiting on to a road, via a metal gate.

Llyn Peris. © Evan Davies

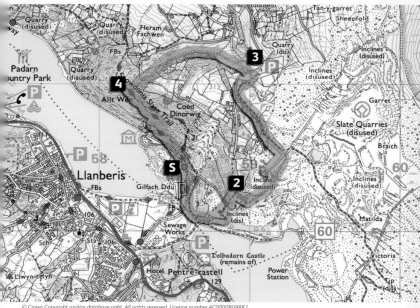

Moel Eilio and Foel Goch from Chwarel Dinorwig. © *Evan Davies*

3 Cross the road (beside a bus turning circle) to access a signposted path through a wooden gate opposite. This path gradually descends towards Coed Dinorwig on a wide track initially. As you enter the trees again, the path narrows; keep a look out for the many tiny gnomes waiting to greet you. About 900m from the road, you will arrive at a junction of paths in woodland. Wooden signposts with a *Snowdonia Slate Trail* marker on them point **left** downhill.

4 Descend the wooded path back towards the National Slate Museum, following zigzags and some tree-root covered sections. After 250m, emerge on to a wider, slate track and **turn right** downhill to a junction of paths and road, and a wooden gate, near the old Quarry Hospital building. **Turn left** through the gate and use the tarmac road to descend to a path junction by an old building. Leave the road here and head downhill towards the Slate Museum car park. Weave through some interesting quarry infrastructure, across the bottom of an old incline with slate carts intact, and emerge at the back of the Llanberis Lake Railway station on the edge of the Slate Museum car park.

/ GOOD TO KNOW

PUBLIC TRANSPORT AND ACCESS

The National Slate Museum is half a mile on foot from Llanberis. Between April and October, there are more frequent bus services to this area via the Sherpa'r Wyddfa bus network. The S1 and S2 buses connect Caernarfon, Betws-y-Coed and Bangor, with connecting services at Pen-y-Pass and Beddgelert. Car users will find parking busy during holidays and weekends, but there are several pay & display options in Llanberis, as well as a car park at the National Slate Museum.

WHEN TO WALK IT

This walk is comfortable in most weather conditions, although its highest point is quite exposed to rain and wind, so it's not a particularly sheltered option for a stormy day. Due to the height gained above Llanberis and the wonderful views towards Yr Wyddfa and Llanberis Pass, it can be a lovely walk to do in the late afternoon or early evening on a summer's day. The 300m elevation reached means that the route can be snow-covered in winter.

TERRAIN AND NAVIGATION

Due to rising interest in visiting the UNESCO site Chwarel Dinorwig, new route signs have been erected at key junctions, and there are some coloured posts marking permissive routes through Coed Dinorwig (owned by Gwynedd Council). This route stays on permissive paths or public footpaths, and there's good reason to do so. Heading off-path into disused quarry areas runs the risk of straying on to complex and hazardous ground, with loose slate and precipitous drops.

FACILITIES AND REFRESHMENTS

Public toilets are available in the National Slate Museum car park. Refreshments are available from the cafe inside the Slate Museum or a refreshment kiosk at the adjacent Llanberis Lake Railway station. There are also numerous options available in Llanberis village itself, including Georgio's Ice Cream shop on the High Street and the always popular Y Pantri cafe as you enter the village from the south-east.

DOGS AND KIDS

This route passes through privately owned land on public footpaths or permissive paths. Hence, dogs are legally required to be under 'close control' but you will see signs asking dogs to be on leads in certain locations. In many places, you won't want your furry friend to go exploring, due to dangers of deep shafts, steep slopes and loose rock. You may see feral goats in the area, and they're not scared of dogs! Children will love this little adventure if provided with some energy-boosting treats for the steep start; take it slow initially; the effort is rewarded.

POINTS OF INTEREST

After the steep start (the zigzags), the route swings right through Dre Newydd (Anglesey Barracks). These cottages once housed quarry workers, who would stay overnight if they lived too far away to walk home after work. You can see the remains of fireplaces and chimneys. Make sure you take a stroll right to the end of the viewing platform at the top level of this walk, which gives breathtaking views towards Yr Wyddfa. When you descend to Coed Dinorwig, you can't fail to be delighted by the cheeky gnomes that you pass …

8.5km / 5.3 miles

02 / NANT PERIS & CHWAREL DINORWIG

A logical and navigable short walk that shows off the impressive landscapes around Llanberis. A wonderful introductory exploration.

/ ESSENTIAL INFO

GRADE ●○○○○
DISTANCE **8.5KM/5.3 MILES**
ASCENT **255M**
TIME **3 HRS (WALKER)/1.5 HRS (RUNNER)**
START/FINISH **NATIONAL SLATE MUSEUM PAY & DISPLAY CAR PARK**
START GRID REF **SH 585 604**
START GPS **53.1218, -4.1153**
OS MAP **OL17 SNOWDON/YR WYDDFA (1:25,000)**

/ OVERVIEW

The unique slate landscapes of this area of north-west Wales have been added to the list of UNESCO World Heritage Sites to celebrate their immense contribution to Wales's cultural and industrial heritage. The expansive quarries of Chwarel Dinorwig produced slate tiles that were shipped all over the world, and this fulfilling route takes in the best aspects of this dramatic backdrop to Llanberis. For those eager to step further back in time, peek inside the early 13th-century fortress of Castell Dolbadarn, built by Gwynedd's Prince Llywelyn Fawr (Llywelyn the Great). Who knew you could span seven centuries of history in a few hours?!

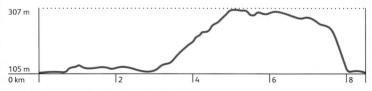

Llyn Padarn and Llanberis from Chwarel Dinorwig. © Evan Davies

Castell Dolbadarn. © Evan Davies

/ DIRECTIONS

S Exit the National Slate Museum car park via the access road, and **keep right** to walk alongside the museum building. Follow the road along to a mini-round-about. **Turn right** and walk 300m along pavement to reach a signposted public footpath to Castell Dolbadarn. **Turn left** down steps to a footbridge over Afon Arddu and follow a path through the woods uphill towards the castle on your left. Keeping the castle on your left, follow a wooded path down a few stony steps towards a wooden gate. Exit this area by way of a short, uphill track to meet the main road (A4086).

2 **Turn left** to follow the A4086 for just over 2km along the shore of Llyn Peris towards the village of Nant Peris. After two sharp bends and a lengthy descent, you will pass a large lay-by on the right-hand side of the road; 200m beyond this, **turn left** on to a tarmac track leading towards the lower sections of Chwarel Dinorwig. After 200m, **keep left** as the track splits between a route to the quarries and a private residence.

3 **Turn left** to pass through a swing gate, accessing a track to the quarries. The tarmac shortly gives way to a slate aggregate trail and this zigzags its way through waste tips up the hillside for just over 1km. Some sections are steeper than others, but the route makes steady progress generally. At 300m in height, the track levels out and passes the huge quarried hole of Twll Mawr (big hole) on your right. Continue for another 1km, descending and ascending again, to reach the even larger galleries and inclines of Chwarel Dinorwig, arriving at a metal swing gate next to an old slate splitting mill.

Mountain goats in Chwarel Dinorwig. © Evan Davies

4 Follow a wide section of path towards a viewpoint, which offers excellent views south-east into the Llanberis Pass and north-west over Llyn Padarn. Retrace your steps back to the long, splitting mill building and **turn left**, following a stony track north-west for 500m, towards an exit to a road through a metal gate.

5 Passing through the gate, keep a field on your left and **turn left** into a narrow, tarmac lane descending for 500m towards buildings. Pass several small cottages on either side before the tarmac gives way to a stony track descending south into the oak woodland of Coed Dinorwig. The path twists and turns round some trees and rocky steps (watch out for tree roots!), arriving at a metal bridge and the ruins of an old drum-house on your right. Continue across the metal bridge and descend more steeply, using a walled, zigzag route, towards the trees below. The final descent to the road is quite steep. There are some wooden steps built into the path to avoid rocky sections. At the bottom of these steps, **turn left** on to a walled section of path that emerges next to a mini-roundabout. **Turn right** here to access the National Slate Museum car park again, 400m away.

/ GOOD TO KNOW

Castell Dolbadarn and Moel Eilio from Chwarel Dinorwig. © Evan Davies

PUBLIC TRANSPORT AND ACCESS

Llanberis village is accessible by bus from various northern locations in Eryri National Park. Use the Sherpa'r Wyddfa bus services, which can help to ease parking logistics in the busy village, especially during peak holiday times. Extra services are available from April to October. The start point of this walk is just under 1km away from the bus interchange (diagonally opposite the Snowdon Mountain Railway station). Drivers can start from the National Slate Museum pay & display car park.

WHEN TO WALK IT

This route is a great half-day option, ideal if arriving or departing from the area. Given the nature of the terrain in the quarry areas (not much shelter from wind and rain), do consider the prevailing weather before setting off, as you gain enough height to feel the effects of wind chill and exposure. During the summer, you could do this walk in the early morning or evening to enjoy the views. This mini adventure is rewarding in most weather and seasons.

TERRAIN AND NAVIGATION

Enjoy clear routes using pavement, aggregate trail, tarmac lane and wooded paths. This journey uses linear features so is quite straightforward for novice navigators, as long as you have the ability to interpret maps and the terrain around you. The slate aggregate trail above Nant Peris takes a zigzag route which removes some of the steepness (though not all!). The final descent back to Llanberis uses a rougher path, with some tree roots and rocky steps to negotiate.

FACILITIES AND REFRESHMENTS

You'll find public toilets in the car park of the National Slate Museum, as well as a cafe inside the museum (free entry to the museum – why not include a visit before or after your walk?). Ice creams are also available at the Llanberis Lake Railway Gilfach Ddu station, next to the car park.

Llanberis village (cafes/shops) is 1km away via an easy trail through the Caer Ddôl meadows beside Llyn Padarn.

POINTS OF INTEREST

Within 1km of the National Slate Museum car park, you can visit the remains of Castell Dolbadarn, owned by Cadw, which is working to protect historic places in Wales. The commanding round tower was built by the Prince of Gwynedd, Llywelyn Fawr and is regarded as one of the most important native-built castles in Wales. At the highest point of this walk, you're surrounded by enormous 'galleries', excavated by decades of quarrying, along with their associated waste tips, inclines for carts and eerie, disused buildings. The scale of the industrial activity is immense.

9.6km / 6 miles

03 / CWM BYCHAN DISCOVERY

A varied walk with upland interest and views of Yr Wyddfa, passing through the village of Beddgelert. Return via the exciting banks of Afon Glaslyn.

/ ESSENTIAL INFO

GRADE ●○○○○
DISTANCE **9.6KM/6 MILES**
ASCENT **315M**
TIME **3.5 HRS (WALKER)/2 HRS (RUNNER)**
START/FINISH **BEDDGELERT**
START GRID REF **SH 588 481**
START GPS **53.0119, -4.1060**
OS MAP **OL17 SNOWDON/YR WYDDFA (1:25,000)**

/ OVERVIEW

Perfect for a shorter day or when there is poor weather on higher summits, this superb family friendly route offers adventures alongside Afon Glaslyn with its well-graded path creeping close to the tumbling waters (handholds are provided where ncessary!) and rewarding views from a gradual ascent of Cwm Bychan. See the eerie remains of copper mine workings, within a landscape which feels quite remote at times. With views of Yr Wyddfa, descend quickly to the popular shores of Llyn Dinas, a perfect picnic spot, and follow a recently improved and fairly level path back to the village of Beddgelert. Ice creams, cafes and shops to suit, and maybe a visit to the legendary grave of Gelert the Dog?

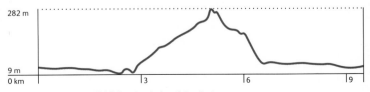

Llyn Gwynant and distant Yr Wyddfa from Cwm Bychan. © Evan Davies

Walking along the Afon Glaslyn.

/ DIRECTIONS

S From the national park car park, or the bus stop on the road nearby, **turn left** and follow the road through the village (passing Glaslyn Ice Cream Parlour on your left) towards a sharp bend left in the road. Do not cross the road bridge here, but walk **straight ahead** for 100m (passing public toilets on your right) to reach a footbridge over Afon Glaslyn. Cross this footbridge and **descend right** on to a path following the river.

2 You're now on a well-marked route (the Fisherman's Path) with Afon Glaslyn on your right. Always keeping the river on the right, follow this path for 2km as it heads towards the steepening sides of the Aberglaslyn gorge. At times the path trends very close to the water, but there you can always find a good footing on stone steps and bridges, and there are even some metal handholds in places!

3 At Pont Aberglaslyn (road bridge), the route **heads left** into trees, following a wooded path for 300m towards a National Trust car park (Nantmor, which has public toilets). Continue under an arched railway bridge and start rising through trees and fields until you reach a gate after 300m. Go through this on to the more open slopes of Cwm Bychan. The route takes a line with rising slopes on either side. Follow the path **north-east** uphill for 2km, passing the interesting remains of copper mine workings. You will also notice a beautifully carved memorial bench; enjoy a moment's rest here with gratitude. After passing some old quarry tips at the 200m contour, ignore any routes to your left and continue along the narrowing valley ahead.

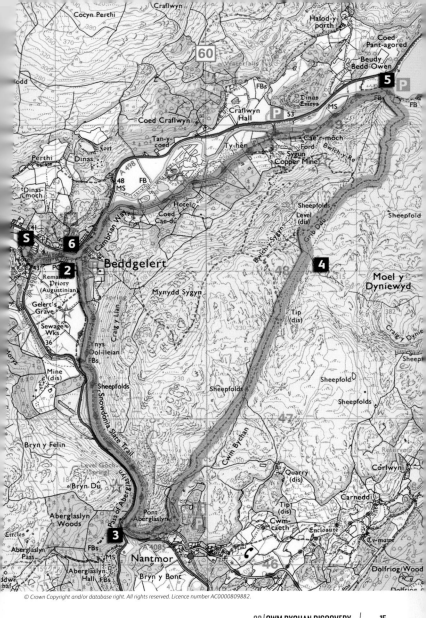

Y Lliwedd and Nantgwynant from Cwm Bychan. © Evan Davies

4 At 282m above sea level, you'll reach your highest point in Cwm Bychan, with excellent views north to Yr Wyddfa and Yr Aran, as well as across to the Moelwynion mountain range. Cross a stile and take the good path **heading left**. This descends towards some old quarry tips, where you **turn right**, heading north-east downhill. The path becomes quite well-pitched as you descend towards Llyn Dinas, zigzagging as the slope steepens towards the lake.

5 **Turn left** along the shores of Llyn Dinas (perhaps after stopping for a picnic). After 200m, you'll reach a gate, which will bring you on to an aggregate path beside Afon Glaslyn. Follow this path for 2.5km back to Beddgelert. The route crosses various fields and uses tracks and a quiet tarmac lane to reach the village. Pass the pretty village green and houses to reach the footbridge where you crossed the river junction earlier.

6 **Head right** over the footbridge towards the welcoming cafes, shops and pubs of Beddgelert. If you have time, you can follow signs to visit the legendary grave of Gelert the Dog, 500m along a good path on the west side of the river.

/ GOOD TO KNOW

PUBLIC TRANSPORT AND ACCESS

Beddgelert is a popular village and can be busy during the summer. As well as the main village car park described here (Eryri National Park – pay & display), there are bus services through the village via the Sherpa'r Wyddfa bus network, which are particularly frequent during the summer. You can travel to Beddgelert by bus from Pen-y-Pass, Porthmadog and Caernarfon, helping to alleviate traffic and parking issues in the village.

WHEN TO WALK IT

This route works in most weathers and at most times of year, even when the higher mountains are very windy or wet/snowy. Do bear in mind that after periods of very high rainfall the path next to Afon Glaslyn can be submerged. The top of Cwm Bychan can be a windy spot when the weather is blowing in from the common south/southwesterly direction, but if you follow this route as described, you'll be ascending with the wind at your back.

TERRAIN AND NAVIGATION

Valley-level paths are signposted from/to Beddgelert. There is a good, visible path for most of the ascent up Cwm Bychan, but it's advisable to keep an eye on location and direction via a paper map and/or mapping devices, especially higher up. Take care when orientating yourself at the top of Cwm Bychan to ensure that you take the correct descent route, as there are a number of other paths and animal trods visible on the ground which may or may not appear on mapping.

FACILITIES AND REFRESHMENTS

Public toilets are available in Beddgelert, as well as numerous shops, pubs and cafes. There is an Eryri National Park Visitor Information Centre near the main car park and a well-placed outdoor gear shop sits by the bridge over Afon Colwyn. Don't miss the extensive flavours of ice cream at Glaslyn – the oldest ice cream parlour in Beddgelert (they also serve great pizzas!).

DOGS AND KIDS

Cwm Bychan sits within Open Access Land. Lawfully, your dog needs to be on a short lead between 1 March and 31 July, which is the breeding season of livestock and ground-nesting birds. This route follows a public footpath, requiring dogs to be under 'close control'. To increase the safety of dogs, animals and people, Eryri National Park advises keeping dogs on leads when walking in upland/farming areas.

This walk would suit capable youngsters, especially the river section. There are options for picnic stops in Cwm Bychan and Llyn Dinas.

POINTS OF INTEREST

Beddgelert is Welsh for 'grave of Gelert,' a dog who belonged to the famous Welsh prince, Llywelyn Fawr. Find out more about the legend of Gelert at the Visitor Information Centre.

Llyn Dinas is one of three sites that are known for being possible homes of the legendary King Arthur's sword, Excalibur; the other two are Llyn Llydaw on Yr Wyddfa and Llyn Ogwen. While walking back to Beddgelert, look out for a wooded, rocky hillside across the Afon Glaslyn. This is Dinas Emrys, reputed to be the final resting place of the mythical white and red dragons.

10km / 6.2 miles

04 / NANTGWYNANT & LLYN GWYNANT

This delightful valley walk can be used to access the waters of Llyn Gwynant for a swim surrounded by ancient woodland, hills and mountains.

/ ESSENTIAL INFO

GRADE ●○○○○

DISTANCE **10KM/6.2 MILES**

ASCENT **260M**

TIME **3 HRS (WALKER)/2 HRS (RUNNER)**

PLUS SWIM TIME

START/FINISH **PONT BETHANIA CAR PARK, NANTGWYNANT**

START GRID REF **SH 627 506**

START GPS **53.0356, -4.0479**

OS MAP **OL17 SNOWDON/YR WYDDFA (1:25,000)**

/ OVERVIEW

Bounded by the steep flanks of Y Lliwedd to the north-west and the more rugged, low-lying hills of the Moelwynion opposite, Nantgwynant is a wonderful valley to explore on foot. With ancient oak woodland and the setting of Llyn Gwynant against a backdrop of Yr Aran and Moel Hebog mountains further south-west, this landscape offers historical links to King Arthur, captured in the 2017 film *King Arthur: Legend of the Sword*. The waters of Llyn Gwynant are a spectacular place to enjoy an outdoor swim in good weather. Please seek further advice for responsible access to water via ***www.adventuresmart.uk/wales***

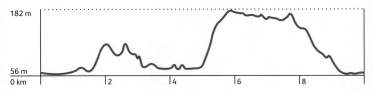

Penmaen-brith (Elephant Rock) across Llyn Gwynant. © D. Osborne/Shutterstock

Looking across Llyn Gwynant to Yr Aran.

| DIRECTIONS

S From the end of the pay & display car park by the public toilets, **turn left** and diagonally cross the A498, heading for a junction with a small lane on your **right**. Use the gate to bypass the cattle grid and walk up the lane for 180m, looking out for a wooden bridge on your **right**. Use the bridge to access a National Trust permissive path that follows a fenceline on your left for 750m, with Afon Glaslyn on your right. Cross a second bridge and follow small permissive path arrows through a gap in a stone wall. **Turn right** and follow a small arrow through a National Trust grazing field to meet a farm track. **Turn right** on to this track and after 550m you'll see a white house 100m from the path on the right. The path swings left and up through a field, passing over spoil heaps from an old copper mine. Descend a grassy path for 400m to a stile, then into woodland, where the path climbs sharply over the ridgeline of Penmaen-brith (Elephant Rock) with a steep rocky drop to the waters of Llyn Gwynant to your right. A couple of rocky steps bring you down the other side of this interesting feature, and the route contours across wooded hillside on a rough path for 800m, before reaching a path junction/stone bridge on your right for Llyn Gwynant Campsite.

2 **Turn right** on to the bridge and enter Llyn Gwynant Campsite, **heading right** after passing through a gate and keeping to a marked public footpath (wooden posts/yellow arrows) that cuts through the campsite towards the shores of Llyn Gwynant, 300m away. As the public footpath leaves the environs of the campsite options emerge to access the water from these eastern shores.

3 The public footpath continues to the main road, where you **turn right** to follow the road for 500m to the next path junction. Take care walking beside this road, which can be busy with parked cars and passing vehicles. After 500m, look out for a gate on your **left** on the opposite side of the road, marked with a public footpath sign. A stony track departs uphill from the gate.

4 **Take care** crossing the road to access the track, then keep a stone wall on your left as you ascend a grassy field. Do not use the privately owned zigzag track; the public footpath keeps to the wall, passing through two gates until a larger field is reached after 500m, and the steepness of the slope eases. Now **bear right**, leaving the stony track and heading into a grassy field instead, where the trod works its way towards an old stone building, passing it closely on the right. Now you are approaching a thickly forested area where the public footpath traces an occasionally muddy route through for 800m. Exit the forest over a stile and follow the footpath along boardwalk sections and a short section through long grass. Continue through grazing fields for 500m, passing a remote house on your left, before crossing a stream at a wooden bridge. Exit on to a lane after another 200m via a gate/stile.

5 This final section uses a quiet lane to return to Pont Bethania. Be aware of blind bends and local traffic. From the gate, **turn right** and follow the lane as it descends, sometimes steeply, towards the valley. After 1.5km, the road makes a sharp turn right to cross Afon Glaslyn and meet the main road. **Turn right** and cross the road to access a lay-by/lane, passing Caffi Gwynant on your left, to reach Pont Bethania car park, 200m beyond the cafe and on your right on the opposite side of road.

/ GOOD TO KNOW

PUBLIC TRANSPORT AND ACCESS

Pont Bethania has become an increasingly popular parking spot in recent years, so the Eryri National Park pay & display car park will be busy at peak times. Consider using the Sherpa'r Wyddfa S4 bus service, which connects with other Sherpa'r Wyddfa buses in the local area. Avoid parking on grass verges to access the waters of Llyn Gwynant; this obstructs the highway and cars may be towed away; this route conveniently accesses the lake on foot.

WHEN TO WALK IT

This route stays at valley level, gaining shelter in woodland at times, so if you don't mind taking to the water in less than perfect conditions, this journey offers a great walk/swim adventure for a cloudy or drizzly day. On sunny summer days you can expect Llyn Gwynant to be busier with other users, but with clever planning you can avoid peak times.

TERRAIN AND NAVIGATION

Low-level navigation through fields and woods can be confusing, so check various resources as you go (paper map, online mapping, footpath signage). Keeping to permissive and public footpaths, with short sections on road, a keen eye will see signs of travel. A few very short sections west of Llyn Gwynant are steep and sometimes muddy, with tree roots covering the path. Be aware of livestock grazing in the National Trust-owned land at the start of the walk.

FACILITIES AND REFRESHMENTS

Public toilets are available at the pay & display car park in Pont Bethania. 200m from the car park is the very popular Caffi Gwynant (contact to check opening times), offering delicious coffee and cake or a more substantial meal and seating inside or out. There are some lovely picnic places on the shores of Llyn Gwynant with excellent valley views, but please remove all traces of litter and food from your break/swim spot.

POINTS OF INTEREST

During the first half of this walk above the shores of Nant Gwynant, the route takes you up and over the recently named Elephant Rock, whose 'elephant' shape will be more visible

Llyn Gwynant from Penmaen-brith.

from the other side of the lake, further round the route. Peering out of the trees at the top of this craggy feature reveals impressive views to the waters of Llyn Gwynant below (beware the steep drops!). The actual name of this rocky band is Penmaen-brith, meaning 'speckled headland'. From afar the rock does look speckled with vegetation and rocky features, and rough like elephant skin.

4km / 2.5 miles

05 / YR WYDDFA – THE HORNS

An engaging and rewarding mountain outing condensed into just 4 kilometres; sample the best Yr Wyddfa (Snowdon) views from unique vantage points above Llyn Llydaw.

/ ESSENTIAL INFO

GRADE ●●○○○
DISTANCE **4KM/2.5 MILES**
ASCENT **280M**
TIME **1.5 HRS (WALKER)/45 MINS (RUNNER)**
START/FINISH **PEN-Y-PASS**
START GRID REF **SH 647 556**
START GPS **53.0805, -4.0207**
OS MAP **OL17 SNOWDON/YR WYDDFA (1:25,000)**

/ OVERVIEW

On the Ordnance Survey map of Yr Wyddfa there is an intriguing reference to 'The Horns' … This undulating ridgeline imposes itself between the north-eastern shores of one of Yr Wyddfa's lakes, Llyn Llydaw, and the bustling Pen-y-Pass. Its modest heights rise above these locations quite superbly, offering a feeling of upland isolation to those who make the effort to gain its grassy slopes, despite its proximity to Pen-y-Pass. You will depart from Yr Wyddfa's main walking routes and find more grassy and boggy ground at times, following fainter paths and sheep trods. This change of character is this walk's appeal, and it is a worthy objective when higher summits are storm-bound or you're short on time.

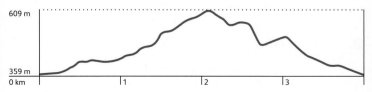

Yr Wyddfa and Crib Goch from The Horns.

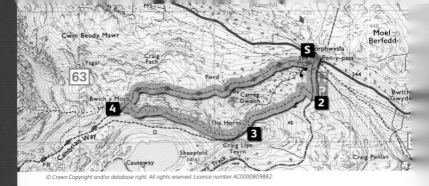

/ DIRECTIONS

S Take a moment at Pen-y-Pass to orientate yourself before leaving the car park! There are signposts near the bus stop area, but you are looking for a wide metal gate on to the Miners' Track (south-east corner of the car park). From this gate, follow the wide track gently uphill for 200m, looking out for a grassy path which leaves the path on your **right**, trending back on itself and ascending the grassy slope above.

2 This less obvious path ascends a generally grassy/boggy/rocky slope, keeping the lumpy top of Carreg Gwalch on your right. Reach a fence boundary at 540m in height. Cross a stile and now keep the fence boundary on your left, **turning left** to progress along the ridge. Carry on for 200m to a lovely, grassy plateau atop the steep slopes of Craig Llyn Teryn (the crag of Llyn Teryn – the smaller lake directly below you, to the south).

3 Walking this route clockwise gives superb views across Llyn Llydaw to the pyramidal summit of Yr Wyddfa. **Turn right** (west) and walk towards the imposing east ridge of Crib Goch. Follow the fence boundary along The Horns ridgeline, using the evident paths on the ground to avoid the steepest rocky lumps. The very undulating 1km along the ridge will absorb quite some time as you work your way through the rugged terrain. You can choose to bypass the final summit top (609m), keeping the high ground on your left as you work around it. After this last, highest summit point on the ridge, a more obvious path descends to a junction of paths at Bwlch y Moch. Here you meet the popular Pyg Track.

4 It's back to reality on the Pyg Track, a very popular path in the summer months. From the junction at Bwlch y Moch (pass of the pigs), **turn right** and use the well-engineered, pitched path to descend back to Pen-y-Pass. This section is 2km long and descends 200m back to the car park; it feels quite tough after all the uphill walking. Save some energy for some steep, rocky steps built into the path.

| GOOD TO KNOW

Pen-y-Pass is a busy place, with a car park, the Yr Wyddfa Warden's Information Office, a cafe and a YHA hostel over the road. It is worth exploring public transport options to Pen-y-Pass, as parking spaces have to be booked in advance (April – October).

The best and most environmentally considerate way to access this location is via the Sherpa'r Wyddfa bus network, which offers regular services to Pen-y-Pass from outlying villages during the summer.

WHEN TO WALK IT

The route is accessible in all but the worst weather. Remember you start 359m above sea level, so the highest sections of The Horns exceed 550m. The ridgeline feels exposed in heavy rain or strong winds, though its aspect can mean that the route is sheltered from the prevailing southwesterly gales by the heights of Yr Wyddfa. The Horns are also very appealing during shorter daylight hours, or as an early morning stroll to catch the sunrise, offering open views to the east.

On the Sherpa'r Wyddfa bus. © John Coefield

TERRAIN AND NAVIGATION

Roughly half of this walk uses Yr Wyddfa's main path, the Pyg Track, in descent (rocky steps and pitched sections of path) as well as a short stint at the beginning on the smooth Miners' Track. The remainder of the route follows fainter tracks across grassy upland terrain, following a fenceline for much of the undulating ridgeline of The Horns themselves. Consequently the navigation isn't overly complex but there are some steep slopes to be aware of, especially above Llyn Llydaw.

FACILITIES AND REFRESHMENTS

Pen-y-Pass has public toilets and a cafe on site, as well as the Yr Wyddfa Warden's Information Office. The YHA hostel, opposite the car park, also has a cafe open to the public at various times. There are few public litter bins at this location; please take your litter home with you, as this eases the pressure on the wardens trying to maintain the site's cleanliness.

POINTS OF INTEREST

Inside the Pen-y-Pass Warden's Office there is a large relief map of the Yr Wyddfa massif which will help to set the scene for your walk, as well as useful maps and local information. From The Horns you can look down on Llyn Llydaw and the long pipeline connecting the reservoir with the Cwm Dyli hydroelectric power station in the Nantgwynant valley below. This pipeline featured in a 'waterslide' scene in the James Bond film *The World Is Not Enough*. In times of very heavy rain and high reservoir levels, the causeway across Llyn Llydaw (the Miners' Track) can be completely submerged.

10.5km / 6.5 miles

06 / YR WYDDFA VIA SNOWDON MOUNTAIN RAILWAY

Combine an upward journey on the historic Snowdon Mountain Railway with an exciting descent route taking in a different aspect of Yr Wyddfa's massif.

/ ESSENTIAL INFO

GRADE ●●○○○
DISTANCE **10.5KM/6.5 MILES**
ASCENT **130M (1,118M DESCENT)**
TIME **3 HRS (WALKER)/1.5 HRS (RUNNER)**
START/FINISH **SNOWDON MOUNTAIN RAILWAY STATION, LLANBERIS (INCLUDING THE TRAIN JOURNEY UP)**
START GRID REF **SH 582 598**
START GPS **53.1164, -4.1194**
OS MAP **OL17 SNOWDON/YR WYDDFA (1:25,000)**

/ OVERVIEW

There's no mistaking the characterful sound and smell of a Snowdon Mountain Railway heritage steam locomotive departing from Llanberis. As steam swells and billows above the station buildings, one can't help feeling that one has been transported back to an age of industrial prestige and excitement, with the impressive sight of the engine pushing its carriages steeply out of Llanberis village. This itinerary of a single rail journey up to Hafod Eryri (the summit visitor centre), a visit to the cairn of Yr Wyddfa and a rewarding descent does require a conducive weather window to get the best views and experience. If you ensure that the planned descent suits everyone in your group, this outing can offer an exhilarating experience, up and down.

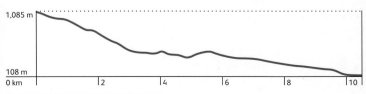

The Snowdon Mountain Railway train by Bwlch Glas.

/ DIRECTIONS

S Exiting the summit visitor centre, **turn left** up stone steps towards Yr Wyddfa's summit cairn. Essential summit photos complete, descend a different set of steps that lead to a stone-pitched path descending north-north-west for 600m beside the line of the railway. This short section brings you to the busy, flat area of Bwlch Glas where the Pyg Track, Llanberis Path and Snowdon Ranger Path meet.

2 Facing north, the railway line will be on your left. **Turn left** and pick up a stony path, descending to the railway and crossing it – this is the Snowdon Ranger Path. You will descend for just under 3km on a clear path throughout, generally heading west-north-west. Above 850m the gradient is easy, giving way to steeper zigzags down to Bwlch Cwm Brwynog. The path is rocky at times but makes excellent downward progress, with pleasing views to the south-west. The slope angle eases again as you reach 450m; continue **straight ahead**, following the level path for 600m towards a metal boundary gate. Go through the gate; another 1km of pleasant walking brings you to a large metal gate with a path junction just beyond.

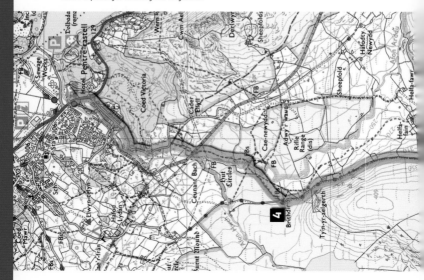

View back to Yr Wyddfa from the old buildings of Cwm Brwynog.

3 **Turn right** on to the public bridleway signed to *Llanberis*, reascending 100m to Bwlch Maesgwm. Follow this newly laid aggregate track up a number of steep zigzags and through a midway gate to another gate at Bwlch Maesgwm. Passing through this gate, follow the path generally north-east downhill for 2.5km, as the route bends round to the left, descending towards an old building on the other side of a gate at the 250m contour.

4 **Turn right** at this old building (marked 'Brithdir' on maps) and go through a metal gate, following a public footpath through fields for 300m to reach a bridge over Afon Arddu. **Keep left** at the path junction after the bridge, following the aggregate track towards gated access to the Snowdon Mountain Railway track crossing. Less than 200m beyond this is a tarmac lane leading down to Llanberis. At the lane **turn left**, passing Pen-y-Ceunant Tea House on the right, before descending quite steeply to a cattle grid/gate at the end of Rhes Fictoria. Continue straight on along the pavement for 300m to a mini-roundabout opposite the Royal Victoria Hotel. **Turn left** here to walk the 150m back to the Snowdon Mountain Railway station.

/ GOOD TO KNOW

PUBLIC TRANSPORT AND ACCESS

Llanberis can be accessed by bus from various locations in northern Eryri. Use the Sherpa'r Wyddfa bus services to ease parking logistics in the busy village, especially during peak holiday times. Extra services are available from April to October. There are numerous pay & display car parks in Llanberis; one of the largest is opposite the Snowdon Mountain Railway, which is the start point of this walk. Please only use designated car parks in the village.

WHEN TO WALK IT

When the Snowdon Mountain Railway is operational! Purchase 'Up Only' single tickets and check that conditions are suitable for your planned descent route for everyone in your group (including youngsters!) At peak holiday times, you'll need to book train tickets in advance; check weather forecasts to help with forward planning and be prepared for the fact that the train may stop before the summit or only

go as far as Clogwyn station if it is very windy.

TERRAIN AND NAVIGATION

This mountain route uses clear navigational strategies, with major path junctions providing clear decision points. Do check your direction of travel from Yr Wyddfa's summit if the visibility is poor (many people walk off down the wrong path!) and check again at Bwlch Glas (a meeting of multiple paths on the descent from the summit area) to ensure that you pick up the Snowdon Ranger Path correctly. Otherwise, the whole route uses clearly identifiable mountain and valley paths, though these do get somewhat rocky at times.

FACILITIES AND REFRESHMENTS

The Snowdon Mountain Railway station offers customer toilets, a licensed Station Buffet and Platform Grill for hot food, snacks, drinks and ice cream, a gift shop and a screen showing specially filmed *Snowdon from Above* footage. If trains are running to the summit visitor centre, there

are additional customer toilets, hot and cold food/drink and a small gift shop there. Do bring your own food and drink for your walk down though, as you can't always rely on the summit cafe being fully stocked.

POINTS OF INTEREST

As your train ascends, before the penultimate station at Clogwyn you'll be able to view the impressively steep cliffs of Clogwyn D'ur Arddu. Upon leaving Clogwyn station, you'll pass the top of a valley called Cwm Hetiau down to your left. When the Snowdon Mountain Railway first opened in 1896, its carriages were open to the elements and blustery mountain winds would sometimes blow the passengers' hats off down the slopes, hence the name Cwm Hetiau (valley of the hats)! On the descent of the Snowdon Ranger Path, the route skirts near the top of Clogwyn Du'r Arddu (take care near the edge!) which offers fabulous views back to Llanberis and the route of the Snowdon Mountain Railway.

15km/9.3 miles

07 / CAPEL CURIG & Y FOEL GOCH

Keeping to quieter slopes, this modest journey offers unrivalled views of Tryfan's eastern aspect and Yr Wyddfa's classic horseshoe. These classic Eryri landscapes are a feast for the eyes.

/ ESSENTIAL INFO

GRADE ●●○○○
DISTANCE **15KM/9.3 MILES**
ASCENT **735M**
TIME **5 HRS (WALKER)/3HRS (RUNNER)**
START/FINISH **CAPEL CURIG**
START GRID REF **SH 720 581**
START GPS **53.1050, -3.9124**
OS MAP **OL17 SNOWDON/YR WYDDFA (1:25,000)**

/ OVERVIEW

If you fancy a change of scene, consider this outing from the village of Capel Curig (meaning 'Curig's chapel'). You'll want to be happy walking over varied terrain and it is sometimes wet underfoot, but if you catch a dry day with good visibility, you'll be rewarded with glorious views of the neighbouring Eryri mountains. Capel Curig offers an excellent base from which to explore various hills and terrain, high and low. This route explores the very eastern tip of the Glyderau massif, as its rocky heights come to rest where the Afon Llugwy and outflow of Llynnau Mymbyr meet. After very heavy rainfall, the low ground of Capel Curig can become dramatically flooded.

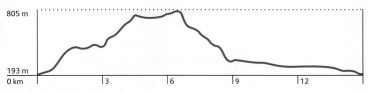

Glyder Fach from Y Foel Goch. © Dan Lane

/ DIRECTIONS

S Find the triangular road junction in Capel Curig (A4086/A5) where this walk commences. Start by following the small lane **north-north-west**, passing to the left of the Joe Brown shop buildings and crossing the Afon Llugwy. The lane rises uphill towards a gate and continues towards a farm building on your left, passing through a second gate. You now face just over 3km of uphill effort, following a small path that weaves through a mixture of broken ground and ferns, before reaching more open terrain. There's no missing this ascent, which rises to your **right** from the farm, Gelli (meaning 'copse/area of trees').

As you strike out on to the Open Access land there is a modest path to follow, heading generally **west**; the ground is steepest in the first 1km. After the 400m contour, the slope angle starts to ease, with undulating walking along Cefn y Capel (the back of the chapel), crossing a wall at the 440m contour.

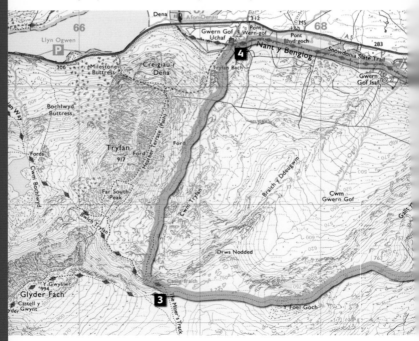

2 There is another wall crossing at the 520m contour; now a distinct change of slope angle rises ahead of you, gaining 250m in height. The way is mostly grassy, with some broken ground; **keep to a boundary wall** for 500m, before the path strikes **west**, gaining height as it heads past large boulders and small crags dotting the hillside towards Y Foel Goch's higher summit area. Approaching the 805m summit, there are steeper slopes down to your right, but the summit ground is quite easy going, albeit dotted with many rocky features standing out from the grass. **Head west** over this peaceful summit, enjoying its panoramic views.

    Descend west down grassy and rocky slopes, passing the waters of Llyn Caseg-fraith. After 1km you'll reach the point (SH 667 582) where a path heads off north (to your **right**), then north-west downhill into Cwm Tryfan. There is a large bulge of rock on the northerly edge of the cwm here.

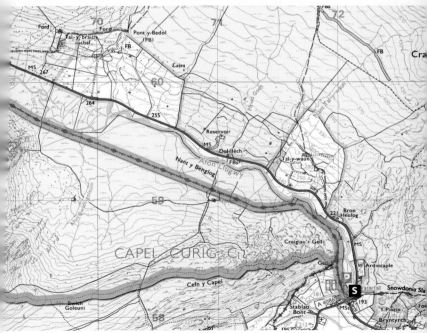

Tryfan from Llyn Caseg-fraith. © Evan Davies

3 The top of the descent route may be tricky to spot initially, but it very quickly becomes much clearer as you **turn left** and the route descends below a bulge of rock. Follow a narrow path down through larger boulders and rocky steps into the head of Cwm Tryfan, with steeper slopes above on your left. This stony path contours across the cwm, heading for the gap below Tryfan's South Ridge (Bwlch Tryfan), but 250m after leaving the ridge, you need to **turn right** downhill into Cwm Tryfan, using a rough path with scree sections.

Below the 650m contour, the ground becomes less steep and you now follow a fairly rough-and-ready path down through the cwm, generally **heading north-north-east**. Tryfan's steep east face is to your left above. Continue on this path for just over 1.5km to a stile over a wall. The next 500m of path tackles a stone-pitched path (sometimes slippery when wet), descending more steeply with the small crag of Tryfan Bach to your left. Emerge on to flatter terrain, where the path leads you in the direction of Gwern Gof Uchaf farm/campsite.

4 Join a significant public bridleway that runs west—east on your side (south) of the farm boundary wall. **Turn right** and use a bridge to cross the river Nant Gwern y Gof. The public bridleway heads east-south-east, following the base of the valley back to Capel Curig, gently undulating at times, but offering an easy return route of about 6km. You will pass through another farm/campsite, Gwern Gof Isaf, and a number of boundary gates. The path can be muddy at times. Emerge at the farm at Gelli, where your walk started, and head back down the lane towards the Capel Curig road junction.

/ GOOD TO KNOW

PUBLIC TRANSPORT AND ACCESS

Between April and October, there are increased Sherpa'r Wyddfa bus services from outlying villages, as well as from Caernarfon, Bangor, Porthmadog and Betws-y-Coed to Capel Curig. Try to use the bus to help ease parking congestion in this small village. There is only one formal car park in the village, located behind Joe Brown's outdoor shop near the walk start point.

WHEN TO WALK IT

If you're happy with the potential of some poor visibility higher up (and using your navigation skills to stay on route), this route could work in conditions when the higher mountains are swathed in cloud or if it's raining. Any mountain route will feel miserable in very high winds and/or rain, but this route does use some sheltered valley paths to descend and return to Capel Curig, and you're not above 700m for too long during the day.

TERRAIN AND NAVIGATION

Expect to find a mix of terrain on this route; low-grade mountain paths (some boggy/muddy areas underfoot), grassy

Track return to Capel Curig.

trods, rocky scree paths and valley trails. If there is low visibility and cloud around the summit height of Y Foel Goch, careful navigation will be required across vague, grassy terrain, before you pick up a much clearer path as you descend into Cwm Tryfan. In both the ascent of Y Foel Goch and the descent of Bwlch Tryfan (and return to Capel Curig), the terrain permits linear navigation following paths and clear landscape features.

FACILITIES AND REFRESHMENTS

There are 'automatic' public toilets just below the Eryri National Park car park in Capel Curig (currently 30p to enter). Don't miss out on a visit to Caffi Siabod, just over 500m south-east along the A5 from the start point; you'll find fantastic home-made cakes and wholesome food,

as well as a reliably friendly welcome. For a more formal meal, the Bryn Tyrch Inn, also along the A5, offers some very refined meals made from locally sourced ingredients.

POINTS OF INTEREST

To the west of Y Foel Goch's summit is an intriguing collection of small llyns (lakes), including Llyn Caseg-fraith (*fraith* means 'speckled'). There's always something slightly eerie about these remote llyns, and their deep sides create a very dark surface, even on the brightest of days. Do stop here for a break with the dramatic backdrop of Tryfan's east face. In descent, pause at the rear of Gwern Gof Uchaf Campsite and its original farm buildings. You can see what this small farmhouse would have looked like in the 19th century.

17km / 10.6 miles

08 / MOEL CYNGHORION

Moel Cynghorion commands attention when viewed from Llanberis, and its quiet expanse is an achievable antidote to its more frequented neighbours.

/ ESSENTIAL INFO

GRADE ●●○○○
DISTANCE **17KM/10.6 MILES**
ASCENT **810M**
TIME **5 HRS (WALKER)/2.5 HRS (RUNNER)**
START/FINISH **LLANBERIS**
START GRID REF **SH 582 598**
START GPS **53.1164, -4.1190**
OS MAP **OL17 SNOWDON/YR WYDDFA (1:25,000)**

/ OVERVIEW

To the south-west of Llanberis village is a graceful, grassy ridgeline; its steep north-western cwms add to its interest. The robust dome of Moel Cynghorion (the hill of the councillors) sits at the south-eastern tip of this skyline, and deserves more attention in its own right. Did this hill and its secret, steep northerly cwms (high valleys) provide an upland meeting place for village councillors in the past? Why up here? The summit gives fine views of Llanberis below, Yr Wyddfa above, and all the way to Ynys Môn (Anglesey) and the coast, and the approach using Bwlch Maesgwm is relatively accessible. So, why not follow in the footsteps of a community and choose Moel Cynghorion for your next hilly conference?

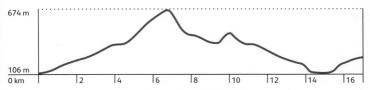

674 m

106 m
0 km   2   4   6   8   10   12   14   16

Moel Hebog and Mynydd Drws-y-coed from the Snowdon Ranger Path. © Evan Davies

Moel Cynghorion with Moel Eilio behind.

| DIRECTIONS

S Standing with your back to the Snowdon Mountain Railway station, **turn right** and walk 150m to cross straight over a mini-roundabout. Use a grassy verge to continue for 170m to a metal gate with a stile over a stone wall on your **right**. Use the stile to access the wide track beyond the gate (public footpath signposted from the road). This track winds up through Coed Victoria for 850m before popping out on a steep tarmac road next to Pen-y-Ceunant Tea House (come back here later!). **Turn left** up the road for 180m looking for a path leaving the road on the **right** at a left-hand bend. Take this aggregate path towards the Snowdon Mountain Railway crossing (gated access over the railway track) and keep following the path through fields on the other side. 450m along this track, **turn right** at a junction and descend towards a wide bridge over the Afon Arddu. After the bridge, **take the left-hand path** across rising fields towards the ruins of a building, labelled 'Brithdir' on the map. Exit the fields via a gate next to this building.

2 **Turn left** up the recently improved track ascending to Bwlch Maesgwm at 467m. It is just over 2.5km to the bwlch (pass), but the route is steady underfoot and gradually gains height, becoming a little steeper at the start and at the very end. Moel Cynghorion is on your left, with some of its steepest slopes visible. Upon reaching Bwlch Maesgwm, views to the south-west open up and you can see towards the Moel Hebog and Nantlle ranges of hills. There are also excellent views towards the summit of Yr Wyddfa to your left.

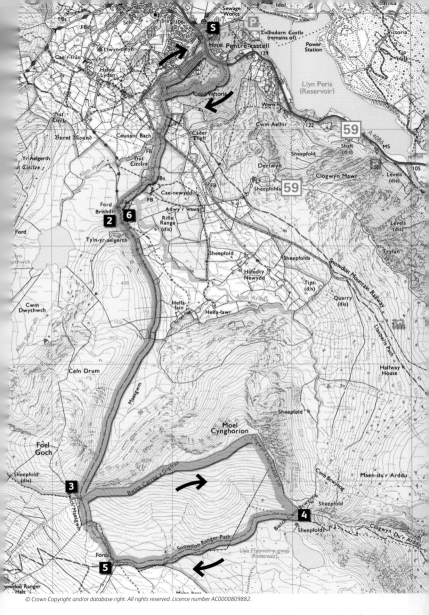

3 Go through the metal gate at the top of Bwlch Maesgwm and **turn left**. You can now see the ascent slope towards Moel Cynghorion's summit. Head up this, always keeping the fence boundary on your left. The slope is steeper for the first 100m of ascent, but above the 600m contour you'll notice the ground eases in angle while still rising towards a flat summit area. On your left are the steeper slopes above Bwlch Maesgwm, emphasising the feeling of height as you look down on to the village of Llanberis and Llyn Padarn beyond. It is just over a mile (1.6km) to the welcome flattening of the modest summit, which is denoted by a small cairn and a stile over the fence. Ignore the stile and keep the fence on your left, **turning right** downhill and **heading south-south-east**, picking up a vague path just beside the fence. There are precipitous crags on the other side of the fence. This steep, grassy section drops quickly to the bwlch (pass) between Moel Cynghorion and Clogwyn Du'r Arddu, the shoulder of Yr Wyddfa.

4 Now at 500m in height, you can drop easily down to the main Snowdon Ranger Path just below you. **Turn right** along this path and follow it steadily for just over a mile (1.6km), going through a gate about halfway along. The path is mostly level for this section and provides lovely walking with open views to the south-west.

5 Pass through a second gate and take the path rising to your **right**, signposted to *Llanberis*. This zigzagging trail is fairly smooth underfoot, but it feels quite steep as it rises to the top of Bwlch Maesgwm again. Go through a gate two-thirds of the way up and continue up the final 250m to regain the top of the pass. Head through the metal gate and enjoy the steady descent down Bwlch Maesgwm, this time with good views of Chwarel Dinorwig (quarries) to the north-east.

6 Reach the old building Brithdir again, **turning right** through a gate to access the public footpath through the fields. **Turn right** over the Afon Arddu bridge, and take the footpath **heading left** back towards the Snowdon Mountain Railway crossing point. The path emerges on to the steep road you used in ascent; don't forget to pop in to Pen-y-Ceunant Tea House now! After the tea house, descend the steep tarmac to a cattle grid and gate at the end of a residential road in Llanberis. Follow this road straight ahead for 300m until you reach the mini-roundabout again. **Turn left** and return to the Snowdon Mountain Railway station and Llanberis village beyond.

| GOOD TO KNOW

View into Cwm Brwynog.

PUBLIC TRANSPORT AND ACCESS

Llanberis can be accessed by bus from various locations in northern Eryri. Use the Sherpa'r Wyddfa bus services to ease parking logistics in the busy village, especially during peak holiday times. Extra services are available from April to October. There are numerous pay & display parking options in Llanberis; one of the largest is opposite the Snowdon Mountain Railway, which is the start point for this walk. Please only use the designated car parks in the village.

WHEN TO WALK IT

This walk could work when higher summits are experiencing poor weather, as the summit is at only 674m. However, the higher elevations of Moel Cynghorion really catch southwesterly winds (though the route direction means you're ascending with the wind at your back). This line of hills can receive snowfall, but due to its lower height and less technical terrain, Moel Cynghorion can provide satisfying winter walking options in good weather. Sunsets seen from its summit are special;

there are excellent views to the west.

TERRAIN AND NAVIGATION

The lower access to Moel Cynghorion is all on navigable and steady paths; the upper part of the route is on smooth grass (steep at times), but the hill shapes are defined and easy to navigate in poor visibility. Hence this walk is graded 'medium' even though it's quite long compared to the other higher mountain walks. Navigation is straightforward, so this is an excellent walk on which to practise your skills.

FACILITIES AND REFRESHMENTS

Llanberis village has plentiful options for eating and drinking – take a walk to the High Street and visit Caffi'r Fran (100 per cent vegan) or Y Pantri for hot drinks, snacks, meals and home-made cakes. Public toilets are located in

Llanberis village or outside Snowdon Mountain Railway when the station is open. On your way back, allow time to pop into the welcoming Pen-y-Ceunant Tea House on the right before your last steep tarmac descent.

POINTS OF INTEREST

After crossing the Snowdon Mountain Railway line in ascent, keep a look out higher on your left for the remains of an old chapel, Capel Hebron. Since medieval times, communities have lived in the high valley of Cwm Brwynog, nestled between Moel Cynghorion and Yr Wyddfa's lower slopes. The chapel was built in 1833 and used until 1958, when the final residents left the area, mostly descending to Llanberis for industrial work opportunities. You'll see the chapel again below on the left, as you ascend the Bwlch Maesgwm path.

10.5km / 6.5 miles

09 / GLYDERAU FROM PEN-Y-PASS

The extensive Glyderau, including the summits of Glyder Fawr and Glyder Fach, stand proudly to the north of Yr Wyddfa – an iconic Eryri mountain landscape.

/ ESSENTIAL INFO

GRADE ●●●○

DISTANCE **10.5KM/6.5 MILES**

ASCENT **850M**

TIME **5 HRS (WALKER)/2.5 HRS (RUNNER)**

START/FINISH **PEN-Y-PASS**

START GRID REF **SH 647 556**

START GPS **53.0805, -4.0207**

OS MAP **OL17 SNOWDON/YR WYDDFA (1:25,000)**

/ OVERVIEW

There are three distinct high mountain ranges in northern Eryri. The most northerly is the Carneddau (the cairns), then the Glyderau, and finally Yr Wyddfa itself. The highest summits of the Glyderau give this rocky massif its name; Glyder derives from the Welsh word *cludair* meaning 'heap of stones'. This lunar landscape is worth exploring, with huge boulders and exciting views towards Yr Wyddfa, especially as you descend to Pen-y-Pass. Walking from the Pen-y-Gwryd Hotel, these dramatic heights are gained more straightforwardly than from the north, using the historic 'Miner's Track' that ascends towards Glyder Fach. This fine route was used by miners commuting to work in Yr Wyddfa's copper mines in the 1800s.

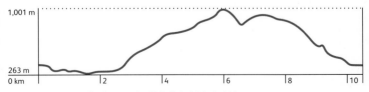

The spectacular Y Gwyliwr (Cantilever stone) on Glyder Fach. © John Coefield

/ DIRECTIONS

S Pen-y-Pass car park is always busy. Carefully negotiating cars, buses and people, cross the car park to the stone wall on the south-eastern perimeter (next to the Warden's Hut). At the bottom corner of the wall you will see a signpost, pointing the way down to the Pen-y-Gwryd Hotel. Go through a swing gate and descend on to a stone-pitched path that avoids walking along a hazardous section of road. Walk downhill for 1.5km, **keeping left/uphill** when you approach another signposted path junction halfway down. Emerge on to the road via a gate, **turn left** and walk uphill towards the Pen-y-Gwryd Hotel, 300m ahead of you. Pass the hotel on your left and follow the road round a right-hand bend for 200m until you reach a stile over a fence on the **left**.

2 Cross the stile and follow a faint path for 200m, heading north-west towards a metal bridge over a stream. Beyond this bridge there is some flatter, usually boggy, ground; head for the stone wall on your left and keep to this wall as you ascend the slope above. An intermittent path (the Miner's Track) keeps the wall on its left and gradually steepens towards another stone wall and stile. You will gain 130m in height to reach this wall.

On the other side of the stile, the ground becomes drier and a rockier, more visible path is gained. Climb steadily upwards in a north-easterly direction to gain another 230m in height and reach a stream with a waterfall above you on the left. Cross the stream using rocks (care will be needed after heavy rainfall) and the rocky path continues uphill, swinging left a little as you gain flatter ground. At 745m in height, you will reach the flattest ground you've been on for a while. Stop and relocate yourself here, as the path can become faint on the soft ground.

3 From this flatter ground, the Miner's Track continues across the plateau to descend north, but your route wends its way to the higher ground now on your **left** – the rocky slopes towards the summit of Glyder Fach. Heading **north-north-west**, pick up a soft trod through grassy ground. This trod becomes more apparent as you start gaining height again – in good visibility you'll be able to see where you need to aim for! Cross the grassy ground for 500m, getting closer to the northern edge of this plateau, before the slope heads more steeply upwards, to your left. As you **turn left** uphill, the ground becomes rockier and a more established path zigzags uphill, with dramatic views of Tryfan on your right.

Ascend another 150m in height until you break through bouldery ground to the rocky plateau of Glyder Fach. Now on flatter ground, **turn left** and head **west-south-west**, slowly gaining height again over boulders and rocks. In poor

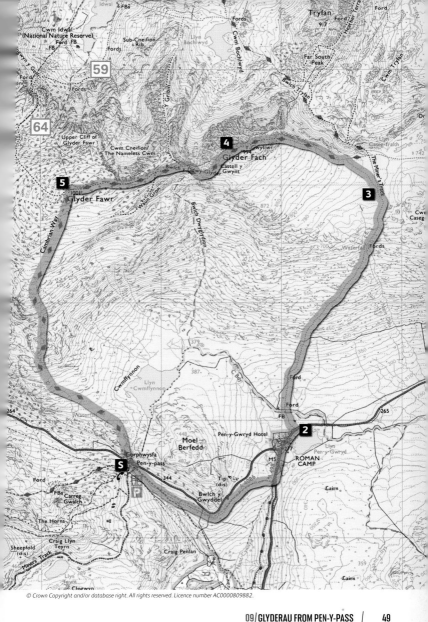

visibility, a compass bearing is useful here. The jumbled collection of boulders on Glyder Fach's summit is only 300m away, and you'll pass the famous Y Gwyliwr (the Cantilever stone) on your left after 200m. The true summit of Glyder Fach is atop high boulders, south-west of Y Gwyliwr. Take care if ascending to this high point for a photo; there are steep drops from some boulders!

4 It is only 1.5km to the next summit of Glyder Fawr, but the rocky path descends to Bwlch y Ddwy-Glyder (the pass of the two Glyderau) first. Keep the seemingly insurmountable Castell y Gwynt (castle of the winds) rock feature on your right, and traverse below it towards the bwlch (pass). A handy path strikes across the slope ahead of you, taking you away from the edge of the rocky cwm on your right and heading left towards Glyder Fawr. Walking **west-south-west**, regain height across grassy and rocky ground, before ascending the final 50m of height to Glyder Fawr's summit, which is a striking collection of upright, slender rocks.

5 The descent from Glyder Fawr's summit offers a wonderful view towards Yr Wyddfa's north-eastern side, including the ridge of Crib Goch (see page 71). Use a rocky path to descend from the stony summit area, **heading south-south-west** for 200m or so until you feel the ground start to ease underfoot into a much gentler slope. You are now following a section of the Cambrian Way down towards Pen-y-Pass; a path is evident in the soft ground and grass ahead. Follow this path for 1km; at this point the broad shoulder you are on starts to steepen to the south-east (your right) and drops away down a series of rocky shelves and crags to the Llanberis Pass below. You are at a height of 750m at this point; it's worth checking a map to relocate, especially in poor weather.

The walkers' route now **heads south,** and you may start to notice some intriguing red painted dots on protruding rocks. These red dots have been historically used as waymarkers and are 'magically' repainted every so often, with many conflicting local stories as to who first painted them. Weaving around rocky outcrops and flatter sections, the intermittent path descends towards a small pool of water at 640m before reaching the top of a stony gully at 600m. Follow a stony path down this shallow gully to gain easier ground. At the bottom of the stony gully, **head south-east** towards the white building of the YHA hostel, just over 1km away. The path becomes more evident through grassy, boggy ground, tracking over (or round to the left – your choice) a final grassy hump before **turning right** more steeply downhill towards the road. Take care crossing the A4086 at the top of the Llanberis Pass – this is possibly the most hazardous section of this route!

Descending past Castell y Gwynt.

PUBLIC TRANSPORT AND ACCESS

Pen-y-Pass is a busy place, with a car park, the Yr Wyddfa Warden's Information Office, a cafe and a YHA hostel over the road. It is worth exploring public transport options to Pen-y-Pass, as parking spaces there have to be booked in advance (April – October).

The best and most environmentally considerate way to access this location is via the Sherpa'r Wyddfa bus network, which offers regular services to Pen-y-Pass from outlying villages during the summer.

WHEN TO WALK IT

A route that's best explored with good visibility on the summits, due to the nature of the terrain on the Glyderau plateau, especially between Glyder Fach and Glyder Fawr, which can be confusing in poor visibility. The Glyderau can also catch early spring snow showers on its plateau. There is not much shelter between the two summits and on a day with a strong southwesterly, you would be walking into the wind. The views are stunning when it's clear!

TERRAIN AND NAVIGATION

The ascent offers straight-forward navigation using the Miner's Track. This puts you on a flatter section of grasses and mosses at 745m. In poor visibility it is crucial to check that you are heading in the right direction towards the final slope of Glyder Fach. Rocks and large boulders litter the Glyderau's summit plateau, offering some interesting walking and great views. Careful navigation may be required to locate each summit and your final descent, especially if visibility is poor in cloud or rain (be aware that conditions can deteriorate quickly!)

FACILITIES AND REFRESHMENTS

Pen-y-Pass has public toilets and a cafe on site, as well as the Yr Wyddfa Warden's Information Office – both open at varied times mid-week and weekends. So long as you leave enough time for your walk afterwards, you could also pop into the Pen-y-Gwryd Hotel

for a quick *panad* (cup of tea) as you pass this famous Eryri hostelry, which was favoured by Everest mountaineers!

POINTS OF INTEREST

Before ascending the Miner's Track, you'll pass the Pen-y-Gwryd Hotel where Sir Edmund Hillary and Sherpa Tenzing stayed while training for their successful 1953 Everest expedition. Behind the ivy-clad walls and windows are wonderful historical photos and memorabilia.

Once atop the boulder-strewn Glyderau plateau, you can't fail to miss the large 'Sentinel' stone – *Y Gwyliwr* in Welsh. This gravity-defying, balanced rock feature, also known as the Cantilever stone, must have come to rest during freeze/thaw and erosion action in the last ice age, well over 12,000 years ago. You can clamber up for impressive photos, but be warned – it can easily be missed in poor visibility!

11.5km / 7.1 miles

10 / FOEL-GOCH & ELIDIR FAWR

Above Nant Peris stand the secretive Foel-goch and Elidir Fawr. Quarrying has marked Elidir Fawr's slopes, but its summit ridge is a quiet delight.

/ ESSENTIAL INFO

GRADE ● ● ● ○
DISTANCE **11.5KM / 7.1 MILES**
ASCENT **960M**
TIME **4 HRS (WALKER) / 2.5 HRS (RUNNER)**
START/FINISH **NANT PERIS**
START GRID REF **SH 606 582**
START GPS **53.1027, -4.0825**
OS MAP **OL17 SNOWDON/YR WYDDFA (1:25,000)**

/ OVERVIEW

At the north-western end of the dramatic Llanberis Pass lies the village of Nant Peris, named after the 'stream of Peris'. The area surrounding the historic buildings of St Peris's Church, the Vaynol Arms pub, the old school, the grade II-listed Capel Rehoboth and the quarry workers' cottages is a Conservation Area and part of Eryri National Park. Rising above the village, the grazed slopes of Foel-goch and Elidir Fawr offer expansive upland walking. You won't see many others on this side! Sneak around the sweeping head of Cwm Dudodyn to access the rockier summit slopes of Elidir Fawr, the mountain with a hydroelectric power station inside it. This fascinating area, marked by centuries of history, is worth exploring.

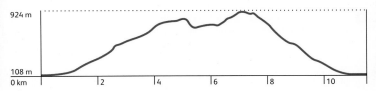

Foel-goch and Elidir Fawr from Yr Wyddfa.

Mynydd Perfedd and Elidir Fawr from Foel-goch. © Evan Davies

/ DIRECTIONS

S Exit the park & ride car park on to the main road (via a walkway near the public toilets) and pause at a wooden gate. You need to **turn left** at this point, but cross the road to gain pavement on the other side. Follow the road for 300m, passing the Vaynol Arms pub on your left, to reach a slatted wooden bridge at a junction with a minor lane. **Turn right** up this lane, passing Tŷ Isaf Farm and campsite on your right and keep following the road steeply uphill for 550m. After a steep bend to the right, **keep left** of the white building ahead of you. The lane keeps ascending less steeply towards a farm building, but look out for a public footpath sign pointing uphill. **Turn right**, ascending the path steeply through rough grazing fields, crossing two stiles, before it zigzags and then bears right round a shoulder of ground, aligning with the Afon Dudodyn below on your left. The path is rockier now and passes a footbridge on your left (you will use this on descent).

2 Continue along the path and through a gate. Ahead of you is the shapely Cwm Dudodyn, but the route ascends more steeply using the shoulder on your **right**. Use a trod through the grass to **ascend east** for 500m towards an old stone wall. Step over the wall; now the ground rises more steeply on to the shoulder of Esgair y Ceunant ('shoulder of the ravine' – although any ravines here-abouts aren't very steep!) following a faint, zigzag route. The going is much easier atop the shoulder, with imposing views of Elidir Fawr to your left.

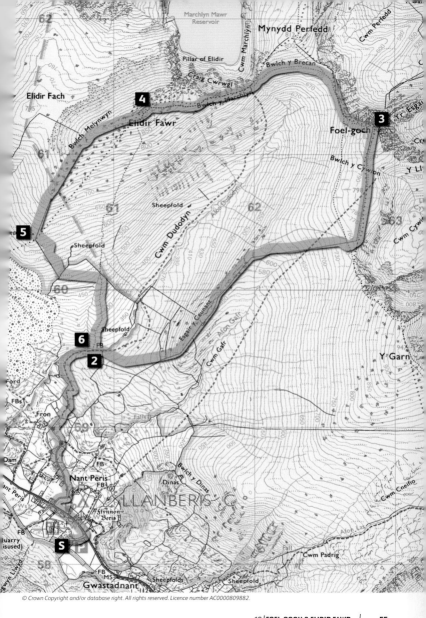

The shoulder extends for 1km; cross a stile across a stone wall after 250m. Ignore a stile on your right, and continue, with a barbed wire fence on your right, until you reach the next stile. Cross this and ascend grassy slopes with the fence now on your left. Gain 150m in height to reach the flatter ridgeline between the summit of Y Garn (on your right) and Foel-goch (left). Cross a stony path to carry on uphill and reach a corner in the fence. **Turn left**, keeping the fence on your left to ascend grassy slopes to Foel-goch summit. Be aware of steeper slopes dropping away to the right.

3 The summit of Foel-goch has an airy feel; be aware of steep drops to the north and east. Use a stile to cross the fenceline and pick up a steep, stony zigzag path, heading **west-north-west** for 100m down to Bwlch y Brecan. Pick up a good path which swings round to the left, steadily ascending for 1km before hitting the rockier slopes of Elidir Fawr. Now heading **west-south-west**, use the stony path to weave through rocky steps, gaining height towards a welcome grassy flattening at 830m. Elidir Fawr's bouldery upper slopes can be seen ahead and the route **continues west** for another 300m, reaching a rocky summit area with a stone wind shelter.

4 From the summit, **continue west-south-west** along the slender, rocky ridge. There are always options to go round larger boulders, usually on your right, to the west of the ridge. Keeping to the ridgeline, continue to descend for 1.5km, with excellent views of Yr Wyddfa and the coast. The ground is fairly rocky underfoot until below the 750m contour, giving way to more broken/grassy ground. Head down to a prominent flatter section in the ridge at the 630m contour. You will see a stone sheepfold here, and an old stone wall to your left.

5 Cross the stone wall without difficulty and **descend south-east** for 300m, quite steeply at times, towards a stile over another wall. There is an intermittent path keeping close to a fenceline on your right, once you've woven through some rocky ground. Cross the stile and **keep left** across the grassy slope, descending gently for 250m to cross a small stream. This will bring you on to a grassy trod on a spur which leads down to Afon Dudodyn and the footbridge you passed in ascent.

6 Cross the footbridge, **turn right** and pick up the path you used in ascent. Zigzag back down through grazing fields, crossing two stiles and descending steeply to a gate leading on to a tarmac road. **Turn left** here and follow the road steeply down past the white house on your left and continue for 500m down to the main road. **Turn left** and walk 300m back to the park & ride car park (or 100m to the Vaynol Arms pub!).

/ GOOD TO KNOW

PUBLIC TRANSPORT AND ACCESS

The S1 Sherpa'r Wyddfa bus service between Llanberis and Pen-y-Pass stops at Nant Peris park & ride car park. The car park has an interactive visitor information system (weather, bus timetables, local information). Nant Peris is 4km from Llanberis High Street so you can also choose to walk along the road, with pavement.

WHEN TO WALK IT

The south-west-facing slopes of these hills are exposed to prevailing winds, but the breeze will be behind you, at least. Enjoying this walk on a quiet summer evening can be rewarding, as Elidir Fawr is one of the Glyderau's most western summits and has wide views west to the horizon, but planning this requires the experience and judgement to make appropriate decisions about 'end of day walking' and attention to the daylight available, pace of travel, and so on.

TERRAIN AND NAVIGATION

The Glyderau massif is characterised by rocky cwms (valleys) and technical ridges, facing north and

Llyn Ogwen and Tryfan from Foel-goch.

east. The slopes down to Nant Peris are smoother and sheep-grazed, and less technical underfoot (except for the summit of Elidir Fawr). In poor visibility, navigation strategies follow defined mountain shapes; you're either going up, along or down. There are hazards to be aware of on any mountain walk, but this Glyderau route is less technical than most.

FACILITIES AND REFRESHMENTS

Nant Peris park & ride car park has public toilets and an interactive information screen at the bus stop (weather, mountain information, bus timetables). There is a welcoming local pub, the Vaynol Arms, in the village, which is open most evenings and during the daytime on weekends, and is worth a visit for local ales and hearty food. Opposite the car park is a popular

farm campsite, Cae Gwyn, which has basic, modern amenities and wonderful views towards Crib Goch.

POINTS OF INTEREST

After leaving the car park in Nant Peris, you'll pass a small chapel on your left, which is dwarfed by the mountains above. This is St Peris's Church, which dates back to the 14th century; it was enlarged over time, and then restored in the 1840s. Residents from nearby Llanberis used to walk to services here before a larger church was built in Llanberis to accommodate the growing population of quarry workers. Beside the chapel is the unassuming base of the Llanberis Mountain Rescue Team. When ascending from the valley, you'll gain a different view over the extensive quarry workings of Chwarel Dinorwig.

14.5km / 9 miles

11 / YR WYDDFA & YR ARAN VIA THE WATKIN PATH

A beautifully rugged walk on Yr Wyddfa. Using the Watkin Path, this challenging route packs a punch in ascent and is worth saving for a special weather window.

/ ESSENTIAL INFO
GRADE ●●●○
DISTANCE **14.5KM/9 MILES**
ASCENT **1,310M**
TIME **5 HRS (WALKER)/3 HRS (RUNNER)**
START/FINISH **PONT BETHANIA CAR PARK, NANTGWYNANT**
START GRID REF **SH 627 506**
START GPS **53.0356, -4.0479**
OS MAP **OL17 SNOWDON/YR WYDDFA (1:25,000)**

/ OVERVIEW
Not content with visiting Wales's highest summit, this circular route also encompasses Yr Wyddfa's easterly aspect and the more modest Yr Aran. Visit Cwm Llan, home to the Watkin Path, the first designated footpath in Britain and a route which offers the greatest ascent gain to the summit of Yr Wyddfa, starting at 57 metres above sea level. Pass the remains of the South Snowdon Slate Quarry, then the section of the path created by Liberal MP and railway developer Edward Watkin in 1892. Watkin's friend and fellow MP, Prime Minister William Gladstone celebrated its opening. You are never far from the impact and history of people on this grand mountain massif. You might even spy damage to the ruined walls of a quarry manager's house. The damage was caused by soldiers' bullets while they trained here during the Second World War.

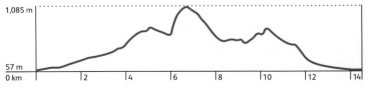

Ascending the Watkin Path, Y Lliwedd in the background. © John Coefield

/ DIRECTIONS

S From the public toilets at the end of the pay & display car park, **turn left** and cross the A498 diagonally, heading for the start of the Watkin Path at the junction of a small lane on your **right**. Go through the gated entrance up stone steps (signed *Llwybr Watkin Path*) and continue easily through oak woodland for 800m, meeting the public footpath marked on maps at a metal gate. **Keep left** round a rocky spur and then **swing right**, climbing towards a second gate. After 2km of walking, the route levels out again at the site of a low weir across Afon Cwm Llan. Just beyond the weir, on your left, is a junction with a path heading left uphill (you will descend this path later).

2 Continue along the wide Watkin Path, crossing a footbridge to head into Cwm Llan and towards old slate quarry workings. 1km beyond the footbridge, the Watkin Path **heads right** and gains height again on a zigzag pitched path through slate tips. The path ascends 450m in height to gain the ridgeline of Bwlch Ciliau, generally climbing north-north-east, with a steeper section of larger rocky features as you approach the ridgeline. **Turn left** at a distinct path junction (to the right is the steep ridgeline of Y Lliwedd). Unless the visibility is very poor, you will see the looming eastern slopes of Yr Wyddfa beckoning you on, as you head north-west along the undulating ridge for 600m on a clear but sometimes rocky path. After reaching a grassy flattening (Bwlch y Saethau), you begin the final ascent towards the summit ridgeline. For the first 300m the path is quite well defined, but as the slope angle increases again, expect some looser rock and eroded sections. Stick to your west-north-west direction, angling across the slope rather than swinging right to climb straight up steep, loose rock. There are a few sketchy-looking shortcut paths here … ignore them! Above 900m in height, you'll find an improved section of pitched path which is firmer underfoot and has more zigzags, simplifying the steeper walking. The pitched path brings you to a large standing stone marking the top of the Watkin Path, and easier ground to your right.

3 **Turn right** and follow what is actually the final section of the Rhyd Ddu Path for 250m to Yr Wyddfa's summit. You will pass the summit visitor centre on your left, before reaching stone steps up to the summit cairn. When you are ready to descend, retrace your steps to the top of the Watkin Path, but then **continue south-west** down the Rhyd Ddu Path along the rocky ridgeline of Bwlch Main for 700m, until you reach the point where the routes split and the Rhyd Ddu Path descends to the right.

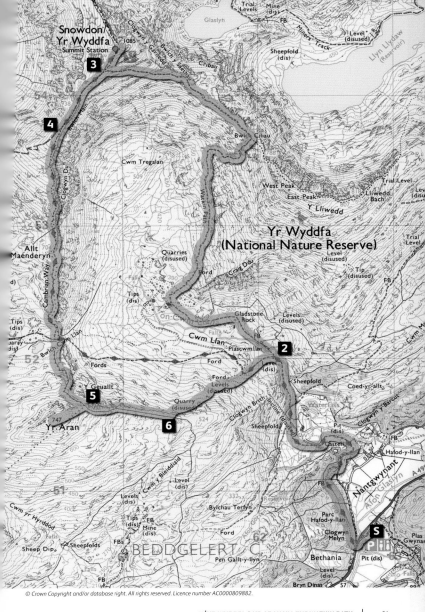

4 Keeping to the crest of the ridge, **continue south** to pick up a path descending Yr Wyddfa's grassy and rocky south ridge for 1.7km, heading for Bwlch Cwm Llan. The path weaves through some steeper sections of rock at times, but the route is well worn and the going is steady. After a final flight of steep, pitched steps, you'll arrive at the flattening of Bwlch Cwm Llan with views across to the Watkin Path to your left. Ahead of you is a short ascent towards Yr Aran. **Keep right** across flatter ground to avoid a large, hidden mine hole in the grassy ground, heading for a stile in a fence at the lowest point of Bwlch Cwm Llan. After crossing the stile, the route ahead generally follows a stone wall up the hill. It is best in this lower section, however, to **keep right** on a grassy slope to work your way around a few steep and wet steps next to the wall, coming back to the wall just below the 550m contour at a distinct corner where the wall swings left. Follow the wall for another 100m in height gain, then **turn left** at a second corner to walk across the slope towards the final ascent of Yr Aran.

5 At the 650m contour at the foot of Yr Aran's north-eastern spur, **turn right** uphill, picking up a rough path following old, intermittent metal fence posts. It's a short walk to Yr Aran's 747m summit. **Retrace your steps**, descending the north-east spur to where a stile crosses the fenceline you followed in ascent. **Turn right** and cross the stile, picking up a rough path descending along Yr Aran's eastern shoulder for 600m, following a wall on your right. At a grassy flattening, look out for a stony path descending to your left at SH 613 515.

6 As you **turn left** down the slope, the top of the path is slightly loose but the angle eases quickly as you make your way down towards more grassy slopes. You are now walking through an old copper mine area; head **north-east** for 700m, picking up a route that heads towards the public footpath descending from Bwlch Cwm Llan. After descending beside a small stream, you'll arrive on an old quarry tramway. Cross this and pick up a more obvious pitched path leading down to the Watkin Path below. At the path junction **turn right** down the Watkin Path, retracing your ascent route, using the route that returns via the woodland path taken in ascent. Once you have reached the road again, **turn right** to check if Caffi Gwynant is open!

/ GOOD TO KNOW

PUBLIC TRANSPORT AND ACCESS

Since the introduction of pre-bookable car parking at the Pen-y-Pass car park, Pont Bethania has increased in popularity as an alternative, so the Eryri National Park pay & display car park will be busy at peak times. To access this quiet valley, consider using the Sherpa'r Wyddfa S4 bus service, which connects with other Sherpa'r Wyddfa buses in the local area. Please avoid parking on grass verges.

WHEN TO WALK IT

Best avoided in wintry snows and high winds; the upper sections of the Watkin Path are steep and can collect a lot of snow, and the southerly descent route does not provide any shelter from the prevailing southwesterly winds. Including Yr Aran's summit is best done with longer daylight hours and stable weather. Starting early offers quieter paths and easier parking, and the route is easy to follow if you head out just before sunrise.

TERRAIN AND NAVIGATION

Yr Wyddfa offers excellent mountain terrain which is steep, dramatic and challenging, but the

Bwlch Main.

popularity of the mountain also means that the path networks are relatively well-defined and managed. Navigation challenges usually come from missing path junctions or turning the wrong way off summits, which can be avoided by taking note of your surroundings and orientating yourself with a map and the features you can see. Steep, stone pitched paths can offer challenges for knees and ankles, especially in descent.

FACILITIES AND REFRESHMENTS

Public toilets are available at the pay & display car park in Pont Bethania. 200m from the car park is the very popular Caffi Gwynant (contact to check opening times). Seating is available inside and out, and you can grab coffee and cake or a more substantial meal. On days when the Snowdon Mountain Railway runs to the summit, you'll find

Yr Wyddfa's visitor centre open, serving hot and cold drinks, snacks and hot food.

POINTS OF INTEREST

Walking through the amphitheatre of Cwm Llan, the Watkin Path passes Gladstone Rock, an outcrop on your left, marked by a marble plaque. In 1892, standing atop this significant dome, surrounded by over 2,000 people, the 83-year-old Prime Minister William Gladstone opened the Watkin Path and thanked the 'people of Eryri' for supporting Liberal MPs to Parliament.

Just before reaching Yr Aran's summit, you'll cross a flat area of grass where an RAF helicopter made an emergency landing in 2016. The crew exited the helicopter safely, but it subsequently caught fire. Scorch marks on the grass were visible for many years after.

13km / 8.1 miles

12 / YR WYDDFA VIA RHYD DDU PATH & SOUTH RIDGE

If you want to explore a different aspect of Yr Wyddfa, head over to Rhyd Ddu for an adventurous approach to Wales's highest mountain.

/ ESSENTIAL INFO

GRADE ●●●○

DISTANCE **13KM/8.1 MILES**

ASCENT **920M**

TIME **5.5 HRS (WALKER)/3 HRS (RUNNER)**

START/FINISH **RHYD DDU STATION**

START GRID REF **SH 570 526**

START GPS **53.0513, -4.1335**

OS MAP **OL17 SNOWDON/YR WYDDFA (1:25,000)**

/ OVERVIEW

West is best? You may well think so when you've explored Yr Wyddfa from this side. This is usually a less-frequented approach, especially outside peak holiday times. The village of Rhyd Ddu is modest in size compared to Betws-y-Coed and Llanberis, but is bursting with character and history, and will not disappoint discerning or hungry walkers. The buildings in the village were mostly built for slate quarry workers and their families in the 1800s, and it's worth checking Welsh Highland Railway timetables to catch a steam train coming through. The upper sections of the Rhyd Ddu Path offer fantastic mountain scenery along Llechog and Bwlch Main, drawing the eye up the expansive and steep western side of Yr Wyddfa.

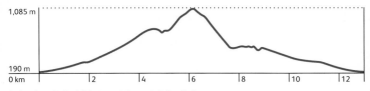

Looking down the South Ridge towards the coast. © Evan Davies

View to Yr Wyddfa from the South Ridge. © Evan Davies

/ DIRECTIONS

S From the pay & display car park, a signpost for *Yr Wyddfa* leads you across the railway line and on to the lower section of the Rhyd Ddu Path. Follow the curving track through farmland for just over 1.5km, and shortly after going through a gate you'll arrive at a distinct crossroads of paths.

2 A waymarker for the Rhyd Ddu Path points **north-east** uphill; follow the stone-pitched path steadily upwards for 1km to a stone wall and gate. The path climbs for another 1km towards the ridgeline of Llechog above 700m. Upon reaching the ridgeline, the path swings to the right, crossing more level ground for 400m before ascending again via zigzags to the start of Bwlch Main at 900m. The next 500m is one of the finest sections of walking path on the mountain, heading along a steep-sided ridge on a steady path which weaves around the vertically lined rocks. When the ridgeline broadens, follow a rocky path for a further 300m, passing the summit visitor centre on your left, before arriving at Yr Wyddfa's summit steps and cairn.

The South Ridge. © John Coefield

3 Retracing your steps from the summit cairn, pass the summit visitor centre again and continue down the steps and rocky path, passing a fingerstone pointing to the Watkin/Rhyd Ddu paths (not easily seen in ascent). **Continue south-west** for 700m along Bwlch Main, reaching a junction of paths at the end of the ridge.

4 On your right is the continuation of the Rhyd Ddu Path used in ascent, but the route instead descends Yr Wyddfa's rugged South Ridge. **Head south**, descending a varied path for 1.5km towards the pass of Bwlch Cwm Llan. The route descends through a steeper section of rock just above the 750m contour.

5 From the flatter, grassy Bwlch Cwm Llan, **turn right** and follow the rocky path heading generally west towards Rhyd Ddu in the valley below. Pass old slate quarry workings and tips, following the line of a railway from the quarry down to the railway station below. After 2km, you'll approach the crossroads of paths seen earlier, continuing **straight on** to return to Rhyd Ddu via the farm track.

/ GOOD TO KNOW

Ascending the lower Rhyd Ddu Path.

PUBLIC TRANSPORT AND ACCESS

To access Rhyd Ddu village, make the most of the Sherpa'r Wyddfa bus services that run around the mountain. Between April and October, services are frequent and the S3 travels between Beddgelert and Caernarfon (linking with other routes via Beddgelert). Car users can park in the Eryri National Park pay & display car park beside the station, but it is more fun to splash out and use the Welsh Highland Railway. Rhyd Ddu station was known as 'Snowdon' in Victorian times.

WHEN TO WALK IT

Routes on this south-western side of Yr Wyddfa do not offer shelter from prevailing southwesterly winds, so walkers can be quite exposed to wind and rain on these routes, in particular on the ridge of Bwlch Main. The walk can be achieved in slightly less time than the longer/more technical options on other sides of Yr Wyddfa. This is advantageous for shorter days in autumn and spring.

TERRAIN AND NAVIGATION

The main paths on Yr Wyddfa are constantly being upgraded and managed. Unless you're seeking out off-path adventures (of which there are many!), you can follow clear, navigable routes from valley to summit. Hence this route uses visible paths on the ground, though the terrain underfoot and mountain conditions can still be challenging at times and keeping track of your location remains essential. The ground becomes more technical above 900m, where the mountain shows off the modest ridgeline of Bwlch Main.

FACILITIES AND REFRESHMENTS

There are public toilets conveniently situated in the pay & display car park.

Do make time for a post-walk visit to the expansive Cwellyn Arms, a traditional and welcoming pub a few hundred metres from the start of the Rhyd Ddu path. Nestled in a row of 200-year-old cottages is the wonderful Ty Mawr Tea House, with a mixture of Danish and Welsh specialities, including amazing pancakes! Both the pub and the tea house offer accommodation too.

POINTS OF INTEREST

Rhyd Ddu is a characterful start point for Yr Wyddfa, used by tourists since the 19th century. Railway operators were desperate for Rhyd Ddu station to become *the* station used to access the mountain, but the mountain railway to the summit was ultimately built from Llanberis. The slender ridge of Bwlch Main is walked twice, giving time to appreciate its dramatic terrain and views into Yr Wyddfa's upper cwms, as well as further south-west to Cardigan Bay. During the descent you'll also pass close to the remains of the Bwlch Cwm Llan slate quarries, cavernous holes dripping with vegetation and water.

12km / 7.5 miles

13 / PEDOL YR WYDDFA / THE SNOWDON HORSESHOE

A highlight among Yr Wyddfa mountain adventures; one to be prepared for in experience and patiently awaited until mountain conditions are ideal. When you're ready, enjoy!

| ESSENTIAL INFO

GRADE ●●●●
DISTANCE **12KM/7.5 MILES**
ASCENT **1,130M**
TIME **7 HRS (WALKER)/4.5 HRS (RUNNER)**
START/FINISH **PEN-Y-PASS**
START GRID REF **SH 647 556**
START GPS **53.0805, -4.0207**
OS MAP **OL17 SNOWDON/YR WYDDFA (1:25,000)**

| OVERVIEW

The finest mountain outing in Wales and, surely, one of the finest in the UK national parks …
For anyone with regular mountain-walking experience and fitness, this beautiful route offers an unrivalled outing over northern Eryri's most iconic mountain terrain – Crib Goch, Garnedd Ugain, Yr Wyddfa and Y Lliwedd. Previous scrambling experience and confidence on exposed and steep rock will increase your enjoyment and chances of completing this route in a day. Planning and patience will be rewarded; this walk tracing the unmistakable, sweeping skyline of Yr Wyddfa demands to be enjoyed to the fullest extent. Waiting for your plans and stable weather and mountain conditions to align will be worth it. The proposed route timings allow for the ascent and scramble along Crib Goch.

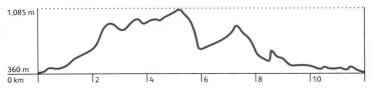

Yr Wyddfa from Crib Goch. © Evan Davies

The ridge of Crib Goch. © John Coefield

/ DIRECTIONS

S Leave Pen-y-Pass car park via the Pyg Track (at the western corner) and follow this well-engineered route for 2km to Bwlch y Moch. The large rocky steps will warm up the legs! Use this ascent to check that mountain and weather conditions are as expected.

2 At Bwlch y Moch pause and think about where you are, the weather conditions and how you're feeling. If in doubt about the intended route over Crib Goch, stay on the Pyg Track towards Yr Wyddfa's summit and rejoin the directions at point 5. If the weather, ground conditions and your group are all positively aligned, then **turn right** at this path junction, ascending towards a stone marker labelled *Crib Goch*. From Bwlch y Moch, there is 352m of ascent to the top of Crib Goch's East Ridge. The East Ridge is the shoulder you can see above you from Bwlch y Moch. A stony path with some rocky steps zigzags up the wider, lower sections, but there are excellent scrambling opportunities above 750m. The more secure and well-travelled rock is always on the crest of the East Ridge, and never on the sides, which are looser and more vegetated. Think 'crest is best'! Above 750m you will see a much steeper rock band; decide now if you're happy to carry on, as it's challenging to downclimb this section if you want to reverse. There are various ways through this band of steeper rock, but you will need to make simple climbing moves to move through this terrain with both your hands and feet on the rock. Look for signs of eroded/scratched rock to keep on the most obvious/easiest line. Above the rock band, there are two more specific rock steps of at least 3m in height that require scrambling to ascend. Again, they are challenging to reverse. Above 850m the crest of the East Ridge starts to narrow and there is a series of broken stone steps that offers steep 'walking' with a need for hands for balance at times. At the top of the East Ridge, you'll see the North Ridge on your right. Where the two ridges join, a slightly flatter area is created where you can rest before the next traverse section.

Ascending the East Ridge of Crib Goch.

3 The next section of the route presents the well-known character of Crib Goch – a very narrow arête that totals 500m in length, with very steep, rocky slopes or crags on either side. To progress with security and confidence, ensure you are well-fed and hydrated, and think about what clothing will keep you at a comfortable temperature; there's not a lot of room on the ridge ahead to attend to 'faff'! Along the first (and narrowest) 180m section of ridge, before the true summit at 923m, there are opportunities to step down to the left of the crest, using the narrow rock as a handrail for your right hand. Always check whether the rocks you are using to steady yourself are secure or loose. There are occasional flatter, wider sections where you can pause. Beyond the summit area, the ridge widens a little and starts to descend slightly towards three pinnacles of rock at the end of the ridge. You can bypass the first two rock pinnacles by keeping them above you on your right (there is more exposed scrambling if you want to ascend over them). The third pinnacle is ascended 'up and over' by a series of steps on the right, as you look at it. It is better to scramble directly over the top than to try to bypass the top via ledges on the right as these are very exposed. Once over the top of the pinnacle, descend by way of a long step down (facing into the rock is easier) and carefully zigzag down broken ground towards the welcome flattening of Bwlch Coch.

4 The next 1.2km of ridgeline towards Garnedd Ugain offers further scrambling opportunities, notably ascending a rocky spur at 950m, but it is always better to stick to the crest of this ridgeline and not be tempted by any paths scooting off to the left to avoid bumps or rocky sections – these notoriously lead to steep scree slopes and nowhere useful. The scrambling on this ridge section is not as exposed as on Crib Goch, and is mostly ascending steep, enclosed

Calm conditions on Crib Goch.

chimneys or large blocks. Emerge near the summit of Garnedd Ugain and on to easier ground above 1,000m. Walk the final few hundred metres to the summit area. Descend south-west on a clear path towards Bwlch Glas and the confluence of paths towards Yr Wyddfa's summit. You will see the railway line coming into view on your right.

> If you need to cut your route short at this point, you can visit the summit of Snowdon and/or descend the Pyg Track from this Bwlch Glas path junction to return to Pen-y-Pass.

 Turn left and follow the railway and final path section for 800m to the summit of Yr Wyddfa. Heading south-west, use stone steps to descend towards the summit visitor centre, passing it on your right as you continue to descend a rocky path to the top of the Watkin Path 250m away. The junction with the Watkin Path is marked by a large stone pillar where you **turn left** downhill on to a steep, stone-pitched path. The upper section of the Watkin Path has recently been re-engineered and offers secure footing down some complex ground, but the lower two-thirds of the path are loose and eroded in places. The route gradually descends across the steep slopes, never heading straight down the stony gullies on the right. Below 850m the ground eases and the path improves, arriving at Bwlch y Saethau and flatter ground. The next 800m of path undulates easily over rocky ground towards another path junction at Bwlch Ciliau (the pass of the corner), where the Watkin Path heads downhill to your right, and Y Lliwedd rises ahead to the south-east.

On the Crib Goch ridgeline.

6 **Continue ahead.** Y Lliwedd looks bold and steep from here, but there is a steady route up that zigzags through the steeper rock bands, avoiding any difficulty. Keep further to the right of the steeper rocks to avoid extra exposure to Y Lliwedd's near-vertical cliff face. Swing too far right, however, and you wander into steeper, awkward, heather-covered terrain. The rocky shoulder is more secure, and the worn route brings you to the top of the West Peak (a narrow path contours round on the southern side if preferred). Y Lliwedd's East Peak is reached after 250m and then the route follows the edge of the ridgeline in descent, arriving at easier ground at the 800m contour. Ahead is the mini summit of Lliwedd Bach; the route continues for 500m over this peak and descends on a defined, sometimes rocky path towards a much broader, grassy area.

7 At a flat, stony area, a cairn marks the point at which the path descends steeply north towards Llyn Llydaw below. **Turn left** at this cairn, looking for a narrow path which diverts left, avoiding a steep, rocky slab. This path zig-zags underneath the rocky slab, before rejoining the main path that steadily descends **north-north-east** for just over 1km, before reaching a junction with the Miners' Track. **Turn right** and follow the Miners' Track easily for just over 2km to Pen-y-Pass.

Between April and October, buses to Pen-y-Pass are increased. Check the Sherpa'r Wyddfa timetables and take a bus to/from Pen-y-Pass or pre-book parking in the Eryri National Park car park, which is possible at a price. You won't be able to just turn up and park, but considering the ascent profile of this route, it is worth planning to start at 359m at Pen-y-Pass.

To enhance your enjoyment and safety on this inspiring mountain route, it is imperative to consider the prevailing weather and mountain conditions. Wait for longer summer days with settled conditions for this one. Look for a wind speed of less than 25mph above 800m; dry rock will increase security underfoot. This walk is described for summer conditions (i.e. no snow); if any sections of the route are snow/ice covered, you should save the outing for another time.

The terrain ranges from well-engineered stone paths and aggregate trail to steep and very

Moel Siabod and Y Lliwedd. © John Coefield

exposed rock steps and ridge sections. Despite the technicality of this route, the general navigation is quite straightforward, following ridgelines and paths for large sections. But the challenge lies in the more detailed route-finding on complex ground over Crib Goch and Y Lliwedd. Experienced walkers will be able to identify where rock has been worn, highlighting the most logical routes, keeping away from more vegetated slopes and loose rock. On both ridges, keeping to the 'crest is best' to find the most solid rock to walk and scramble on.

By starting and finishing at Pen-y-Pass you benefit from access to the Warden's Office and mountain route and weather information, as well as public toilets and a choice of cafe options within the warden's building or across the road

at YHA Snowdon Pen-y-Pass. Pen-y-Pass is generally busy, especially at weekends during the summer, and is extremely busy on sunny bank holidays. Be strategic about when you plan to do this walk!

At Bwlch y Moch (the pass of the pigs), you can discern the Yr Wyddfa horseshoe route, as well as Llyn Llydaw reservoir and its outflow pipe, which delivers water to the Cwm Dyli hydroelectric power station below. The pipe was used in exterior filming for the James Bond film *The World is Not Enough*; there are no pipeline bombs here now! Jumping from action hero to Arthurian legend, Bwlch y Saethau (the pass of the arrows) on the ridgeline between Yr Wyddfa and Y Lliwedd is said to be the site of King Arthur's last battle with his nephew, Mordred.

21km / 13 miles

14 / YR WYDDFA SKYLINE

A grand parade across a shapely skyline of summits above the village of Llanberis. Walk Yr Wyddfa and its neighbours in one long day.

/ ESSENTIAL INFO

GRADE ●●●●
DISTANCE **21KM/13 MILES**
ASCENT **1,550M**
TIME **7 HRS (WALKER)/4 HRS (RUNNER)**
START/FINISH **LLANBERIS CAR PARK SOUTH OF LLYN PADARN**
START GRID REF **SH 579 602**
START GPS **53.1204, -4.1243**
OS MAP **OL17 SNOWDON/YR WYDDFA (1:25,000)**

/ OVERVIEW

A 'big round' is very satisfying; starting and finishing from a logical valley location and tracing the surrounding skyline. While there's much merit in making Yr Wyddfa the sole focus of a day's walk, this route offers an extended adventure, worth saving for when time, weather, fitness and motivation all align. Moreover, Yr Wyddfa is not the only star of this scenic parade; there's also the enjoyment of the approach along the Moel Eilio range, with rocky heights beckoning you onwards. You might question this as you ascend the Snowdon Ranger Path's zigzags, but if you're armed with many snacks and have the time to pause and take it all in, you can make the most of a longer day out.

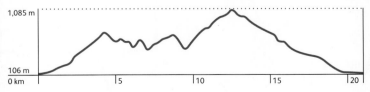

Yr Wyddfa summit. © John Coefield

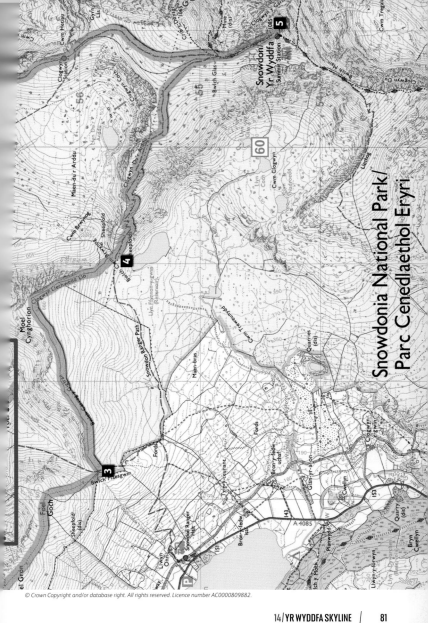

Snowdon/
Yr Wyddfa
Summit Station

Snowdonia National Park/
Parc Cenedlaethol Eryri

/ DIRECTIONS

S Look for the play park adjacent to the pay & display car park south of Llyn Padarn. From the park, cross the road at the pedestrian crossing and take a short, pedestrianised lane towards Llanberis High Street. At the top of the lane, **turn left** and walk 200m to the junction of Fford Capel Coch. **Turn right** up this street and follow it for 1.5km, passing a school on your left, before the road steepens to pass YHA Llanberis. The road continues to climb, passing through a gate at Hafod Lydan farm buildings and continuing to a second metal gate, where the tarmac ends. **Turn right** on to a public bridleway, soon crossing a stile/gate and heading uphill for 200m to reach another gate.

2 Go through this boundary gate and **turn left** uphill, ascending through boggy ground to reach a stile. Climb steeply at first to gain a grassy ridgeline that leads south-west towards Moel Eilio's summit. The slope angle eases after the 350m contour. 300m from the summit, you'll notice a path joining you from the right (north). Keep the fenceline on your right now and follow it to the flat summit area and stone shelter. From Moel Eilio's stone shelter, head **south-south-east** and descend to a stile over a stone wall. There are steeper slopes on your left now, but ahead of you is 2.5km of glorious hillside, descending and re-ascending over two more summits, Foel Gron and Foel Goch, and heading generally south-east all the while. The final descent to Bwlch Maesgwm is rather steep, with a stepped path giving the feet some purchase.

 An excellent public bridleway descends north-north-east from Bwlch Maesgwm towards Llanberis if you don't wish to ascend further.

3 From Bwlch Maesgwm, **turn left** through a boundary gate and **turn left** again, uphill, keeping a stone wall and fence on your left as you ascend the grassy slopes of Moel Cynghorion. You are only 1.5km away from the summit area, and the ground becomes less steep above the 600m contour. (You could omit this summit by descending south-south-east from Bwlch Maesgwm, down a public bridleway path instead. This path meets the Snowdon Ranger Path (turn left where the paths meet and follow the Snowdon Ranger Path to Bwlch Cwm Brwynog, through a number of gates).) Your ascent route generally heads north-east until you reach the modest flat summit, where there is a stile over a fence. Keeping a fence on your left, **head south-south-east** down a steepening grassy slope with an intermittent path towards Bwlch Cwm Brwynog.

 Yr Wyddfa skyline and Moel Eilio.

4 Rising from Bwlch Cwm Brwynog is the imposing ridge of Clogwyn Du'r Arddu. Pick up the Snowdon Ranger Path heading **east-south-east** and ascend its rocky zigzags for just over 1km to reach a welcome, easier slope above 850m.

> If an early exit is needed from this point, you can instead follow the Snowdon Ranger Path as it descends south-west towards a junction with the Bwlch Maesgwm public bridleway and a return to Llanberis.

Follow the path for 1km and cross the Snowdon Mountain Railway track, before reaching a stony flattening at Bwlch Glas (the junction of the Llanberis Path, Pyg Track and Snowdon Ranger Path). **Turn right** at a large finger-stone, using the wide, stony path next to the railway line to access Yr Wyddfa's summit. This final section of path is just over 600m in length and is usually busy with people, dogs and trains!

5 From the stone steps at Yr Wyddfa's summit, retrace your route back to Bwlch Glas. Be sure to take the correct path in descent – do not ascend any paths to your right (leading to Crib Goch), but keep level to pick up the Llanberis Path heading north. This path is wide and stony, passing the low ruins of a stable building on the left after 300m. Continue to descend a steeper, rocky section

Llanberis Path descent.

of path above Clogwyn station for 1km. Take care – this can be loose and is an accident black spot for the Llanberis Mountain Rescue Team. **Turn left** under the railway bridge just before Clogwyn station and then leave the Llanberis Path, **turning right** to gain ground next to the railway line again. Keeping the railway line on your right, you'll arrive at Clogwyn station on a flat area of grassy ground. Continue to descend gently along grassy slopes with the railway line on your right for 1km, sometimes weaving in and out of rockier ground. After 1km the railway line sweeps round to the left and downhill.

6 Cross the railway line here and start to descend open ground. Keeping the railway line on your left now, pick up an intermittent path that descends towards the main Llanberis Path below you. **Heading west**, walk downhill for 500m and drop on to the Llanberis Path near to the Halfway House building. Follow the obvious Llanberis path steadily downhill for a further 2.5km, **turning right** when you exit on to a steep, tarmac lane.

7 Drop height quickly on this lane, passing the Pen-y-Ceunant Tea House on your right (an excellent refreshment point!). Another steep section of tarmac after the tea house brings you down to a cattle grid and on to Rhes Fictoria. Keep to the pavement on this busy road and after 50m, **turn left** at a road junction and go under an impressive arched bridge of the Snowdon Mountain Railway. You are now on Church Road. Ignore any lanes leaving this quiet road and follow the road gradually round to the right, passing houses and an old church. After 600m you'll reach Llanberis High Street. **Turn left** to access shops and amenities in the village. Opposite the Spar you'll see the pedestrianised lane leading back to the play park and the car park.

| GOOD TO KNOW

PUBLIC TRANSPORT AND ACCESS

Between April and October, there are increased bus services from outlying villages and towns including Caernarfon, Bangor, Porthmadog and Betws-y-Coed to Llanberis. Check the Sherpa'r Wyddfa timetables to help ease parking congestion in this busy village. For car users, there are numerous pay & display car parks in the village; this route starts from the car park next to the public playground south of Llyn Padarn. Please only use designated car parks, rather than residential parking.

WHEN TO WALK IT

Given the distance/ascent of this route, and its focus on summits, plan this route for late spring/summer days with a good amount of daylight. Look for a stable weather forecast for the duration of your walk; good visibility will allow you to enjoy the views on this high-level series of summits. If tackling it during shorter daylight hours, some morning darkness can be tolerated for the first part of the route out of Llanberis village.

View south from Bwlch Maesgwm. © Evan Davies

TERRAIN AND NAVIGATION

This route offers a good mix of terrain underfoot, offering interest all day, and keeping away from particularly boggy ground (except for the lowest slope of Moel Eilio, which is distinctly wet at times!). Enjoy lower village lanes and tracks, grassy hills, aggregate trails and rockier sections of mountain path. As this route follows hilly ridges and summits (at times on clear paths), the navigation is quite straightforward so long as directions of travel are understood when on high ground.

FACILITIES AND REFRESHMENTS

The walk starts from Llanberis and depending on your timings there are various options for food/drink, though fewer for very early risers (you'll probably find yourself in the local Spar!). At the end of the day, you'll pass the quaint and cosy Pen-y-Ceunant Tea House and full dinners can be found at the Padarn Hotel on Llanberis High Street. There are public toilets across the road from the walk start at the pay & display car park.

POINTS OF INTEREST

At the bwlch (gap) between Moel Cynghorion and the ascent of the Snowdon Ranger Path up Yr Wyddfa, pause at a stile over a fence to peer into Cwm Brwynog and across to the Llanberis Path on the other side. Cwm Brwynog was the remote home of a small community of quarry workers and smallholders, who lived here without electricity or telephones until the 1950s. While descending the Llanberis Path, before reaching Clogwyn station, take a look into Cwm Hetiau (the valley of the hats), where strong winds would whip hats from Victorian railway passengers and blow them down the mountain!

23km / 14.3 miles

15 / TOUR OF YR WYDDFA

Explore Yr Wyddfa's varied massif using a network of connecting public footpaths; this route still packs a punch in terms of ascent, despite not visiting any summits!

/ ESSENTIAL INFO

GRADE ●●●●
DISTANCE **23KM/14.3 MILES**
ASCENT **1,190M**
TIME **6 HRS (WALKER)/3 HRS (RUNNER)**
START/FINISH **LLANBERIS BUS INTERCHANGE**
START GRID REF **SH 581 599**
START GPS **53.1173, -4.1200**
OS MAP **OL17 SNOWDON/YR WYDDFA (1:25,000)**

/ OVERVIEW

Each aspect of Yr Wyddfa offers varied valleys, landscapes, history and human stories from the Bronze Age, the Industrial Revolution and present-day communities. This intriguing route is almost a complete circle, with a scenic bus journey connecting the start and finish through the dramatic Llanberis Pass. The route is described anticlockwise to work with the terrain, but could be reversed if desired. It takes a little imagination and planning to achieve a longer, hilly walk without touching any summits – and this is it. Striking an effective balance between rugged and simple terrain, while keeping to a lower elevation overall, this journey gives Yr Wyddfa the opportunity to show off its many different aspects and landscapes.

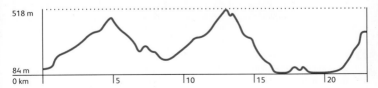

Yr Aran from Rhyd Ddu. © Matt Elliott/Shutterstock

/ DIRECTIONS

S With your back to the bus interchange shelters, **head diagonally left** towards the Snowdon Mountain Railway station and continue along the road, passing the station building on your right, towards a mini-roundabout. **Turn right** at the roundabout, following Rhes Fictoria to where the road crosses a cattle grid and climbs steeply. Ascend the road, passing Pen-y-Ceunant Tea House on your left, and look out for a stony path leaving the road on the right, 100m after the cafe. **Turn right** on to this path, crossing the mountain railway and continue for 400m, descending to a wide footbridge. **Turn left** on to a path ascending gently through fields and walk another 400m to reach an old building, going through the gate next to it.

2 **Turn left** at the building and start ascending a well-engineered, aggregate track towards Bwlch Maesgwm, 2.5km away. This section is straightforward to walk, passing through a couple of gates and enjoying a flatter section in the middle, before a steepening towards the bwlch (gap). At the top, **head straight** through a boundary gate and descend the clear path on the other side for 600m, sweeping round bends and zigzags, to a path junction. **Turn left** and immediately go through a metal gate. Look out for a stile over a stone wall, a short distance away from the path and less than 50m beyond the gate.

3 Cross the stile and enter a series of fields, descending for 1.5km towards an old quarry area. Waymarkers keep walkers on track across the grassy ground, and some of the ground is quite wet underfoot at times. Use a narrow bridge over Afon Treweunydd to cross an impressive waterfall, before circling round to your left beneath old slate quarry tips (some wet ground). The path makes a distinct **turn left** uphill, using an old quarry incline to wiggle through this area. Descending out of the quarry the other side, you're now 1.5km from Rhyd Ddu with some mixed ground to cover, including more wet grass! Nearer Rhyd Ddu you will pick up an improved track leading down to the valley. When you arrive behind houses in the village of Rhyd Ddu, follow *public footpath* signs towards Rhyd Ddu station. There are public toilets in the station car park if needed.

 The S3 Sherpa'r Wyddfa bus route links Rhyd Ddu with Caernarfon and Beddgelert if transport from the valley is needed.

4 A signpost for *Yr Wyddfa* leads you across the railway line and on to the lower section of the Rhyd Ddu Path. Follow this track through farmland for just over 1.5km until, shortly after going through a gate, you arrive at a distinct crossroads of paths. Leave the Rhydd Ddu path and **continue east**, taking

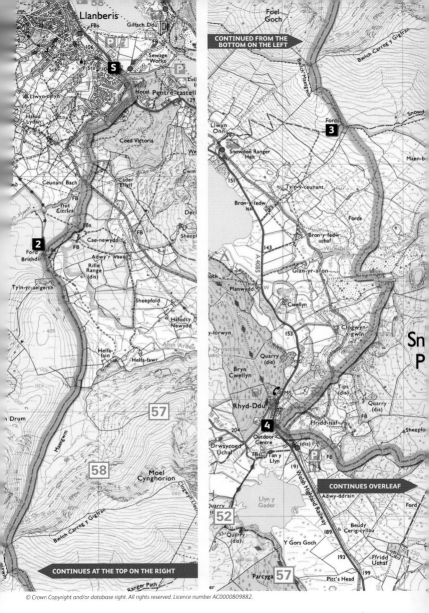

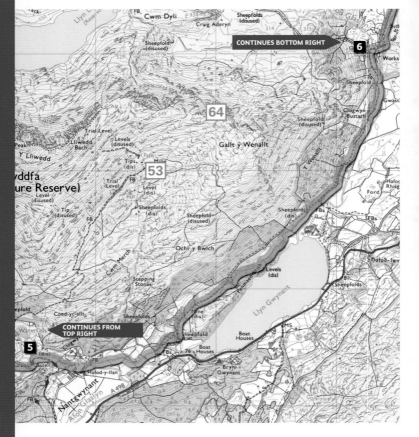

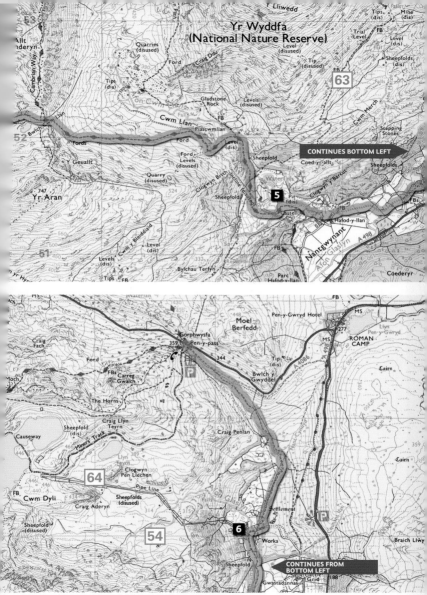

a track that steadily climbs for just over 2km towards Bwlch Cwm Llan. This path is an old tramway route that brought slate from Bwlch Cwm Llan quarries to Rhyd Ddu. After reaching the top of the bwlch, descend the other side more steeply, on loose stones initially, to pick up a better route gently descending generally east for 2km into the wide base of Cwm Llan. This path is quite grassy and soft underfoot at times and meets a level tramway track from the South Snowdon quarry tips. Follow this for 200m to a junction where the tramway carries on ahead, but the route **heads left** downhill, using a pitched stone path to join the main Watkin Path below. At the junction with the Watkin Path **turn right**, heading steadily downhill and passing through a gate. Follow the path round a sweeping bend to the left for 700m and as the path swings right again, look out for a small waymarker pointing to a smaller path, which leads downhill to your **left**.

5 The permissive path descends beside Afon Cwm Llan through National Trust land towards the campsite of Hafod y Llan, a National Trust farm. Go through a gate to campsite fields and farm buildings, then exit on to a farm track and **turn left** towards a vehicle bridge. On the other side of the bridge, pick up a vehicle track/permissive path through fields (usually containing cows and/or sheep). The route stays low-level for the next 4km, but travels through some varied terrain. About 600m after the bridge, you'll reach a white house away from the path on the right; here the path **swings left** and up through a field over spoil heaps from an old copper mine. Descend a grassy path for 400m to a stile then into woodland, where the path climbs sharply over the ridgeline of Penmaen-brith, with the waters of Llyn Gwynant below steep rock walls to your right. Descend a couple of rocky steps on the other side of this interesting feature, and contour across wooded hillside on a rough path for 800m until you reach a path junction and a bridge on your right to Llyn Gwynant Campsite. Do not cross the river but continue through fields for 1.5km to the large Cwm Dyli hydroelectric power station.

6 The public footpath **swings right** and crosses a footbridge over Afon Glaslyn at the northern edge of the building. Head through a gate, then **turn left** to access the continuation of the public footpath through another gate. The track is a well-defined aggregate path again, staying level for 700m to a footbridge over Afon Trawsnant. Now the route begins to climb the final 1.2km up to Pen-y-Pass on a mixture of stone-pitched path and grassy sections. Just over halfway up, the path merges with a route ascending from the right; continue steadily along the rocky path towards the Pen-y-Pass car park. At a swing gate, exit into the car park, where you'll find the bus stop and facilities.

/ GOOD TO KNOW

PUBLIC TRANSPORT AND ACCESS

This route works best if you utilise the Sherpa'r Wyddfa bus network, accessible from various villages in northern Eryri. Starting at the Llanberis Bus Interchange, the walk culminates at Pen-y-Pass, where buses can be boarded to return to Llanberis, Caenarfon, Betws-y-Coed, Beddgelert or Porthmadog. The route could be walked in reverse if that suits bus schedules better but the way described is best in terms of ascent/descent. Walk green!

WHEN TO WALK IT

This route offers an exciting exploration of lower terrain, yet still accumulates a lot of ascent through the day, even though the highest elevation reached is only 500m while going 'up and over' certain passes. It is also a good option when hazardous weather conditions, or snow and ice, are present on higher elevations in winter, though bus services will be limited in this season. If walking the route in autumn/winter, the first section is relatively straightforward to navigate during darkness, making a much-needed early start easier to plan for.

View north from Bwlch Maesgwm towards Llanberis. © Evan Davies

TERRAIN AND NAVIGATION

In recent years, Eryri National Park have worked to connect and improve the public footpaths that encircle Yr Wyddfa. Some route sections or junctions are waymarked by signposts and, apart from a notorious boggy section above Rhyd Ddu station, the paths are clear and navigable.

FACILITIES AND REFRESHMENTS

There are public toilets on the Llanberis High Street (400m from the start), as well as cafes and shops. Alternatively, make time for a *panad* (cup of tea) at Pen-y-Ceunant Tea House on the steep, tarmac road above Llanberis. There are also cafe options at the finish at Pen-y-Pass, either inside the Warden's Office building (where there are also public toilets) or at the bar inside YHA Snowdon

Pen-y-Pass, which are open at various times.

POINTS OF INTEREST

Descending from Bwlch Maesgwm, you'll arrive at Rhyd Ddu station. Built in 1881, this remote platform now serves the Welsh Highland Railway, but the line used to carry slate towards Caernarfon, connecting with the London and North Western Railway network. In the late 1880s, Rhyd Ddu *almost* became the station for Snowdon, until landowners and railway entrepreneurs opted for Llanberis. Before ascending to Pen-y-Pass, visit Cwm Dyli, a hydroelectric power station built in 1905. At the time it was the largest hydroelectric station in Britain, drawing its water from Llyn Llydaw on Snowdon via a large pipe down the hillside.

/ APPENDIX

TOURIST INFORMATION

/ *www.visitsnowdonia.info* – tourism information

/ *www.snowdonia.gov.wales* – national park website, with tourism, conservation, travel and car park information

/ *www.visitwales.com/destinations/north-wales* – inspiring information for Eryri and beyond

SELECTED PUBS, CAFES & PLACES TO STAY

There are any number of good places to eat, drink and stay near Yr Wyddfa. The following is just a selection. For more info, visit the websites listed above.

/ **Vaynol Arms**, Nant Peris
www.robinsonsbrewery.com .... **T** 01286 871 624

/ **Becws Melyn Bakery/Cafe**, Llanberis
www.instagram.com/melyncafebakerybar .... **T** 07546 232 909

/ **Caffi Caban**, Brynefail
www.caban-cyf.org .... **T** 01286 685 500

/ **Caffi Gwynant**, Nantgwynant
www.cafesnowdon.co.uk .... **T** 01766 890 855

/ **Garth Farm Campsite**, near Capel Curig
www.garthfarmcampsite.co.uk .... **T** 01690 720 212

/ **YHA Snowdon Pen-y-Pass**
www.yha.org.uk .... **T** 0345 371 9534

/ **Cwellyn Arms**, Rhyd Ddu
www.snowdoninn.co.uk .... **T** 01766 890 321

/ **Plas Coch Guest House**, Llanberis
www.plascochsnowdonia.co.uk .... **T** 01286 872 122

GEAR SHOPS

/ **V12 Outdoor**, Llanberis
www.v12outdoor.com

/ **Joe Brown**, Llanberis and Capel Curig
www.climbers-shop.com

/ **Crib Goch Outdoor**, Llanberis and Beddgelert
www.cribgochoutdoor.com

/ **Alpkit**, Betws-y-Coed
www.alpkit.com

MOUNTAIN WEATHER

Both the Mountain Weather Information Service and the Met Office provide dedicated mountain forecast for Eryri (Snowdonia) National Park.

| **www.mwis.org.uk**
| **www.metoffice.gov.uk** – forecast for summits and key places

USEFUL WEBSITES

| **www.sherparwyddfa.wales** – info about the Sherpa'r Wyddfa bus service
| **www.climb-snowdon.co.uk** – useful info and planning for Yr Wyddfa
| **www.adventuresmart.uk/wales** – general planning and safety information
| **www.llechi.cymru** – UNESCO Slate Landscape of North-west Wales
| **www.snowdoniaslatetrail.org** – waymarked valley walking routes

ABOUT THE AUTHOR

Kate Worthington is a qualified Mountain Leader, Winter Mountain Leader, UK Athletics Fell and Trail Run Leader, and British Nordic Walking Instructor, based in Eryri (Snowdonia). She provides walking and run guiding and skills training through her business, RAW Adventures, and has experience of guiding large and small groups in the UK mountains and overseas, from corporate teams, youth groups and runners preparing for mountain races and events. She is a regular contributor of routes to *TRAIL* magazine, and lives in Nant Peris at the foot of Yr Wyddfa with her husband, daughter and collie dog, Nonny.

Based in Eryri, RAW Adventures has been owned and operated by Kate and Ross Worthington since 2008. We love working with small and large groups of all ages and abilities. We work with qualified and trusted Mountain Leaders and instructors to offer a range of activities for you, your family, friends and colleagues.

We love to plan bespoke adventures, as well as offering more well-known routes and summit days. Our office base is near Llanberis, close to Yr Wyddfa. It is a hub of activity and always open for a coffee and chat ...

This is Eryri. This is Snowdonia. A beautiful national park offering rich rewards to those who stay awhile and are keen to learn more about its quiet corners and cwms, as well as its majestic mountaintops. Visit Wales and let us help plan a unique adventure.

www.raw-adventures.co.uk

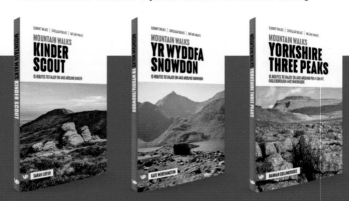